AF772201

Voicing Responsible AI Pedagogy for Music and Visual Arts Education

Lauri Väkevä

Voicing Responsible AI Pedagogy for Music and Visual Arts Education

palgrave
macmillan

Lauri Väkevä
University of Helsinki
Helsinki, Finland

ISBN 978-3-031-86412-4 ISBN 978-3-031-86410-0 (eBook)
https://doi.org/10.1007/978-3-031-86410-0

This Palgrave Macmillan imprint is published by the registered company Springer Nature Switzerland AG.
The registered company address is: Gewerbestrasse 11, 6330 Cham, Switzerland

Preface

Like any work examining cutting-edge technologies, this book will inevitably become outdated. Analyzing a moving target is challenging enough, and it becomes even more so when the target's destination remains unknown. This is precisely the situation we face with Generative Artificial Intelligence (GenAI) in the arts.

While we can speculate about AI's general trajectory, uncertainty persists regarding how these possibilities will shape creative pursuits. Will AI transform how we make, share, and experience art? Could it even reshape our aesthetic sensibilities and tastes? Might AI create art that rivals—or exceeds—human creation? Could AI itself become an art form? What do these questions mean for education as it grapples with both present cultural realities and future technological developments? In the age of AI, who teaches, who and what do they teach, how, and on what (and whose) conditions? As AI becomes an active participant in education, what factors—and whose interests—guide our pedagogical choices? And ultimately, does this benefit the profession?

In texts exploring AI's engagement with culturally significant practices, authors often deploy GenAI to articulate ideas about its capabilities. In the preface to my previous book, I used a then-contemporary version of a popular large language model (LLM) to interpret a dream that inspired that work's final touches. In retrospect, using an LLM for dream interpretation seemed particularly apt, given these models' well-documented tendencies to hallucinate or 'confabulate.' This parallel becomes especially timely when considering the operational principles behind today's content creation models.

Like many colleagues, I have been experimenting with AI for creative and educational purposes since it became user-friendly with the launch of the first GenAI chatbots in 2022. While the use of AI is not new in artistic and scientific contexts, chatbots like ChatGPT have made it easy to incorporate GenAI into the creative work processes. With the increasing availability of GenAI models designed to produce creative content in various forms—and across different content modes—one can confidently say that their use is becoming ubiquitous.

Through my involvement in academic in-service training and workshops focused on GenAI, I have noted a pressing need to develop pedagogically sustainable approaches to AI usage. As many colleagues have pointed out, these approaches require critical AI literacy, which includes several components that go beyond mere technical proficiency.

One premise of the following text is that a crucial aspect of this literacy should be pedagogical sustainability. Furthermore, it is emphasized here that the arts provide particularly interesting contexts for developing critical AI literacy, as in them, one can experiment freely with the generative capabilities of the latest models in relatively safe environments, concentrating on their creative possibilities. However, such free-form experimentation should not be done at the cost of recognizing the risks of AI use.

Since the 2010s, GenAI has evolved from experimental technology to widespread tool for creative industries, bridging different art forms and providing new possibilities for transdisciplinary education and study. As its influence expands, we need critical dialogue about its potential and limitations. Rather than offering definitive answers to how GenAI should be implemented in the classroom, this book aims to spark discussion about its prospects and risks and give ideas for developing critical AI literacy among teachers and students in the arts, specifically in the context of visual and auditory expression. Whether you are an artist, educator, or policymaker, the questions raised here will hopefully challenge you to reconsider technology's role in shaping the future of the arts within and outside educational contexts.

The chapters of this book explore the evolving relationship between GenAI and visual and auditory arts from a variety of perspectives, emphasizing a pedagogical angle. The book opens with an introduction that clarifies its key concepts and establishes the philosophical framework of what follows. It then situates its primary theme of voicing within this framework by examining voice cloning and its potential impact on aesthetic spaces, followed by an analysis of sustainability issues surrounding the use of GenAI in pedagogical contexts. The text then reviews GenAI's multimodal possibilities, proposing a transdisciplinary approach to its study. After exploring how GenAI challenges traditional didactic approaches to education in and between the arts, the book proceeds with a discussion of the unique polytemporality that digital technology—and particularly GenAI—brings to artistic practice. The conclusion synthesizes these insights and outlines future prospects.

Competing Interests The author has no competing interests to declare that are relevant to the content of this manuscript.

Helsinki, Finland Lauri Väkevä

Contents

CHAPTER 1

Introduction

Abstract This introductory chapter offers conceptual clarifications and outlines the philosophical foundation supporting the following exploration. It discusses key concepts, including art(s), education and Bildung, transformation, GenAI, AI (as) art, late modernity, and voicing. The philosophical framework merges a critical approach to studying technology with pragmatism in a posthumanist context.

Keywords Art education • *Bildung* • Artificial intelligence • Late modernity • Voicing • Pragmatism • Posthumanism

This book examines the integration of Generative Artificial Intelligence (GenAI) into art(s) education. The text explores both the transformative potential and associated risks of this disruptive technology, proposing criteria for assessing its pedagogical relevance in artistic and inter-artistic contexts of late modernity. The aim is to advance critical approaches to studying GenAI using the cultural phenomenon of *voicing* as a thematic anchor. This introductory chapter provides some conceptual clarifications and outlines the philosophical foundations that underpin the subsequent exploration.

L. Väkevä, *Voicing Responsible AI Pedagogy for Music and Visual Arts Education*, https://doi.org/10.1007/978-3-031-86410-0_1

Art(s)

While this book explores topics relevant to all arts, it mainly focuses on ideas and practices related to music, sound, and visual expression. This emphasis stems from the author's lifelong fascination with how visual and auditory phenomena can illuminate and educate shared human experience.

Yet the approach of this book rests on the premise that certain features are common to all arts. These shared elements typically include—but are not limited to—expression, imagination, creativity, materiality, communication, and aesthetic value. While art forms utilize these elements differently, instances of them can be found in various artistic disciplines. Throughout this book, when it is necessary to emphasize art as both singular and plural, the somewhat awkward term 'art(s)' is used (see also Väkevä 2023a). Thus, art(s) education indicates here education within and across the arts.

Education and *Bildung*

In this book, 'education' extends beyond the mere transmission of knowledge, skills, and attitudes from teachers to students. Drawing from the continental European pedagogical tradition, education is here conceptualized as a multifaceted and intricate system of purposeful—and often institutionalized—actions that aim to foster learning, human growth, and what Germans term *Bildung*: a lifelong journey of becoming a self-reliant individual capable of navigating the complex physical, cultural, and social milieux that characterize modern (and late modern) life.

While theories of *Bildung* vary (see, e.g., Siljander et al. 2012; Sjöström and Eilks 2021), this book emphasizes its ethical implications. Through *Bildung*, we evolve as resilient, reflective, and responsible agents inclined to treat others with dignity. *Bildung* thus also implies *Sittlichkeit*: an ethical disposition essential for full and sustainable participation in a society's culture (Miettinen 2020). Though this book does not advocate for any specific ethical-political framework, it acknowledges that democratic and egalitarian societies provide more fertile ground for cultivating such a disposition than alternative systems.

Transformation

The noun 'transformation' and the adjective 'transformative' in this context refer to education's capacity to foster human growth and *Bildung*, not only by changing those who are educated but also by altering the conditions of their agency. This does not necessarily imply an overhaul of one's previous disposition—though that can occur. Often, the changes are subtle, such as developing new ways of seeing, hearing, and listening.

Art can also transform subtly. As Jacques Rancière (2004) argues, it can even be considered transgressive on account of its capability to refashion the 'distribution of the sensible'—our sensory encounter with the world and how we share it as aesthetically meaningful. These ideas are explored further below when examining GenAI's potential to reshape aesthetic experience. For now, it is crucial to note that GenAI, like all technologies, should be evaluated in art(s) education based on its ability to transform our relationships with the world and each other.

GenAI

GenAI refers to self-adaptive digital technologies that harness artificial intelligence (AI) for creative purposes, emulating human intelligence. As of Fall 2024, when this introduction was written, such technologies were epitomized by multimodal large language models (MLLMs) capable of generating content across various formats. Some experts argue that the development of such models may make it virtually impossible to differentiate between human and machine-made output, forcing us to reconsider the role of machines in creative domains (see, e.g., Danesi 2024; Miller 2019).

Moreover, the rapid advancement of GenAI may blur the line between AI-produced content that *represents* and that which merely *presents*. The question of whether GenAI is an epistemic agent that can be judged on account of how it represents reality remains questionable. Some critics regard GenAI as a mere 'stochastic parrot' capable only of statistically predicting desired content (Bender et al. 2021). However, taking GenAI merely as a statistic prediction mechanism overlooks its hallucinating or 'confabulating' abilities—its capacity to generate new content by filling in gaps, which sometimes produces surprising results (Ramsøy 2024; Sui et al. 2024). Whether this ability qualifies GenAI as a genuinely creative artistic force capable of composing—rather than just generating—artworks is a central question explored in this book.

AI (as) Art

The use of AI in the arts is not a new thing, with experiments dating back to the 1960s (Audry 2021; Miller 2019; Zylinska 2020). Today, AI is used to support creativity in all art forms, and the techniques of applying GenAI to artistic purposes are developing at a rapid pace as its models become more sophisticated (Danesi 2024). Some commentators even argue that the recent advancements of GenAI have the potential to transform existing artistic approaches due to its expanding human-like capabilities (Voigts et al. 2024a). Some go even further than this and suggest that GenAI is approximating an art form in itself, which means that it would need to be judged on its own aesthetic terms (Voigts et al. 2024b). This raises the question of whether it provides more than a tool to support artistic work processes (cf. Lanier 2023).

Be that as it may, as the first quartile of the twenty-first century comes to a close, GenAI is ostensibly developing a potential to influence the whole cycle of how we make, share, exchange, and appreciate art and commit to other creative pursuits. This influence indicates that AI continues to shape our "cultural and aesthetic practices," perhaps with the power even to "revolutionize" the whole "field of cultural production" (Voigts et al. 2024b, 14). A central claim of this book is that the increasing presence of GenAI in creative processes and practices of cultural production should be critically examined by art(s) educators.

Late Modernity

'Late modernity' refers here to the notion that 'high modernity'—a twentieth-century social-ethical-economic order built on expectations of efficient work distribution, perpetual growth, and functional social institutions—has faced unforeseen challenges in today's world of global crises and wicked problems (Bauman 2000; Beck 1992; Giddens 1997; Reckwitz 2017, 2020a, 2021). These crises and problems indicate an emerging need to reinterpret modernity's core principles of self-reflection—such as what it means to be a human being and what it takes to live harmoniously with others and the rest of the world.

One way to illustrate the late modern condition is to examine how industrial economies transformed into post-industrial economies in the latter half of the twentieth century. This shift automated many tasks that previously required human labor (Bell 1976; Giddens 1997; Touraine

1971). Today, we find ourselves in a situation where several occupations risk losing their meaning as human pursuits entirely, as cutting-edge AI offers unparalleled possibilities for workflow automation. Whether this will significantly impact the arts and cultural production remains to be seen. At the time of writing this, there seems to be a consensus that AI automation may not lead to substantial job displacement in creative professions. Yet, it is likely to disrupt these fields in ways that necessitate that creatives learn to work alongside it (Hatzius et al. 2023).

A more contemporaneous perspective on late modernity recognizes creativity as a valuable asset in the virtual markets of distinction. This recognition is based on a sociological theory, according to which economic shifts have led to a society that increasingly puts cultural emphasis on creativity, with individuals seeking recognition as characters of unique disposition (Reckwitz 2017). Many are now willing to invest considerable time and energy into showcasing their lives as worthy of attention on social media and other digital platforms, to which adaptive digital technologies provide support in exchange for collecting their user data (Reckwitz 2020a, 2020b). At the same time, many others feel culturally displaced and unable to enjoy the benefits of the new global value order, which leads to political unrest and social polarization (Reckwitz 2021).

One central premise of the present book is that art and education are not immune to such economic, societal, and cultural changes but can either maintain or resist them. In addition, self-adaptive digital technologies, such as GenAI, play an increasingly important role in shaping how educational systems, practices, and values both reflect and reinforce the transformations in late modernity, and art(s) educators should recognize their impact on their occupation.[1]

Voicing

Voicing has been defined in various ways in different disciplinary contexts (see, e.g., Baxter 2011; Beville 2009; Borrows and McNeil 2022; Bray and Bray 2013; Bruhn 2002; Looby 1996; Nasukawa 2005; Nazneen and

[1] It is also possible to recognize a late modern form of art that aesthetically reflects how modernity has been moving into its latest phase. The author has analyzed the implications of this possibility in a previous publication, arguing for the importance of its recognition in art(s) education (Väkevä 2023a). The present text continues the earlier discussion by suggesting that Gen AI introduces new creative ways to engage with late modern culture, ways that should be acknowledged and critically studied by art(s) educators.

Maheen 2014). While acknowledging a variety of interests behind these definitions, this book draws on their common threads, addressing this phenomenon at several levels of agency, both human and non-human.

On a personal level, voicing can refer to gaining, having, and using a voice that is expressive, communicative, distinctive, contextual, identity-bearing, and/or meaningful. It may also involve taking a stand or position in relation to other voices, thereby situating its user within the shared world. Thus, voicing can also be viewed as a means of carving out a unique place in a social-cultural context.

Voicing can be thus discussed as an expression of human subjectivity, identity, or uniqueness or as a relation to others. While voicing can be understood in terms of subjectification—allegedly a cornerstone of *Bildung*—this book emphasizes its relational nature, aligning with Mikhail Bakhtin's (1983) point that a voice always orients toward other voices. Thus, voicing indicates the possibility of dialogical relations, where individual 'voicers' aspire not merely to be heard but also to be listened to, which makes voicing a political effort (see also Rancière 1999). However, one could also argue that voicing can take place without intention or positionality; in this case, it could be examined as a matter of *performativity*. Performativity is discussed more thoroughly later; at this point, it suffices to say that it refers to the potential of voicing to make changes in the shared world, which does not necessitate a human agent.

Following these preliminary conceptual clarifications, a philosophical context is now outlined that provides an argumentative framework for the subsequent discussion.

A Critical Approach to Studying Technology in Educational Praxis

The following pages address the need to develop innovative AI art(s) pedagogies for late modern societies and cultures. This book aims to meet this need by critically examining GenAI in art(s) education—its possibilities and hazards. While not intended as a didactic handbook, the text hopefully offers insights into how to integrate GenAI into teaching praxis.

'Praxis' in this context refers to a critical and self-reflective way of doing things together. It is a form of social action that is able to constantly observe its conditions, remaining alert to the potential need for adjustment. While praxis has been discussed in various ways in philosophical and educational literature (see, e.g., Arendt 1989; Carr and Kemmis 1986; Freire 1985; Grundy 1987; Kemmis and Smith 2008), this book views it as an inherently reflective and critical practice that aims for the best outcomes for the persons involved. Thus, praxis always implicates an ethical element.

This perspective helps us to witness GenAI not merely as a technical innovation but as a disruptive technology that calls for critical reflection on its development, use, and applicability when applied in critical praxis. 'Disruptive' here implies more than GenAI's ability to alter existing practices. Aligning with critical studies of technology, this book considers GenAI as a catalyst for transforming technologically mediated praxes rather than simply a set of technical solutions confined within existing value frameworks. As a disruptive technology, its potential to transform human lives needs to be recognized as an ethical question, especially when examined in the context of education that aims to support *Bildung*.[2]

In this light, GenAI is not merely a technological product but presents itself as a discipline, science, and an approach—and maybe even an art form—that helps us explore how technological solutions to emerging challenges can foster or impede *Bildung* in educational praxis. This means that its disruption is not necessarily harmful unless one does not accept the need for change. This study aims to strike a balance between technological optimism and skepticism by adopting a pragmatic yet critical stance. Such an approach seeks to facilitate a dynamic, inclusive, and ethically alert exploration of GenAI's transformative potential in art(s) education within late modernity while remaining alert to its possible adverse effects.

Developing Critical Pragmatism in a Posthumanist Context

This book's argument draws primarily from a combination of critical pragmatist and posthumanist philosophies. Two key figures stand out here: John Dewey and Karen Barad.

[2] Stiegler (2019) uses the term 'disruption' to refer to the effects of technological innovation on societies, economies, and individual consciousness. Disruption can even involve a breakdown of the structures that sustain social practices. Here, the term is used to point out the transformative power of GenAI, which can manifest in different areas of society and culture, including the arts.

Despite their different academic backgrounds and the generational gap between them, both of these philosophical figures emphasize the importance of developing a systemic worldview without reducing its complexity to the scope of scientific research. While both maybe can be considered *philosophical naturalists*—as they are both inspired by science and seek philosophical solutions in line with scientific inquiry—they also seem to acknowledge the limitations of science in providing answers to existential questions. In this sense, they maybe can be both characterized as 'soft' or 'cultural' naturalists, in contrast to 'hard' naturalists who tend to reduce philosophical problems to scientific ones (see, e.g., Dolphijn and Tuin 2012; Godfrey-Smith 2002; Hickman 2013; Rouse 2004; Shook 2017; Väkevä 2007, 2012, 2023a).

Both Dewey and Barad also seem interested in developing philosophical views to address ethical issues while maintaining an understanding of the significance of advancing social praxes based on democratic values. Thus, both seem determined to make things significantly better for future generations, which justifies discussing their work in the context of educational philosophy. Indeed, educationalists have used both philosophers' ideas as frames of reference. Dewey's position as a key developer of modern (and, as I argue, late modern) educational philosophy is well known. However, Barad's ideas have increasingly gained momentum in educational discourses, especially in connection to feminist scholarship.[3]

In essence, this book argues that, despite their differences, Dewey and Barad together offer building blocks for constructing a viable philosophical framework for exploring GenAI integration in art(s) education. This integration also aligns with the broader ethical goal of bolstering various forms of sustainability—an aim that shapes much of today's educational discourse for obvious reasons.

As it is understood here, sustainability encompasses the three pillars of the Brundtland report (Report of the World Commission on Environment and Development: Our Common Future 1987)—environmental, economic, and social—but also embraces cultural, technological, political, aesthetic, and maybe even pedagogical dimensions (see below). The idea

[3] Barad has also been described as a feminist naturalist, in line with the problem-setting background of their philosophy (Rouse 2004). For feminist re-readings of Dewey, see Seigfried (2001); Vorsino (2015). While not an exercise in feminist philosophizing, this book acknowledges the importance of feminist value basis in developing posthumanist frames of reference.

is here that linking Deweyan pragmatism with Baradian posthumanism enables us to navigate the complex implications of GenAI in art(s) education, allowing us to be both responsive and farsighted in relation to its disruptive potential in the late modern pedagogical spaces where art is taught and learned and, hopefully, *Bildung* takes place. Indeed, Dewey viewed a critical approach to technology as essential for fostering political mindsets conducive to democratic ways of life (see Hickman 1992, 2001). In turn, Barad (2003, 2006) suggests that building critical mindsets requires perspectives that challenge modern anthropocentric solutions to traditional philosophical problems. Together, these thinkers guide us to examine technologies as crucial elements in constructing what Biesta (2022) characterizes as a world-centered education: an education that brings people into dialogue with the world without the need to occupy its center. What this means in terms of human-AI-relationships provides an essential refrain for the present discussion.

References

Arendt, Hannah. 1989. *The Human Condition*. Chicago, IL: University of Chicago Press.

Audry, Sofian. 2021. *Art in the Age of Learning Machines*. Cambridge, MA: The MIT Press.

Bakhtin, Mikhail M. 1983. *The Dialogic Imagination: Four Essays by M. M. Bakhtin*. Austin, TX: University of Texas Press.

Barad, Karen. 2003. Posthumanist Performativity: Toward an Understanding of How Matter Comes to Matter. *Signs: Journal of Women in Culture and Society* 28 (3): 801–831. https://doi.org/10.1086/345321.

Barad, Karen. 2006. *Meeting the Universe Halfway: Quantum Physics and the Entanglement of Matter and Meaning*. Durham, NC: Duke University Press. https://doi.org/10.1215/9780822388128.

Bauman, Zygmunt. 2000. *Liquid Modernity*. Cambridge: Polity.

Baxter, Lesile A., ed. 2011. *Voicing Relationships: A Dialogic Perspective*. Thousand Oaks, CA: Sage.

Beck, Ulrich. 1992. *Risk Society: Towards a New Modernity*. Thousand Oaks, CA: Sage.

Bell, Daniel. 1976. The Coming of the Post-Industrial Society. *The Educational Forum* 40 (4): 574–579. https://doi.org/10.1080/00131727609336501.

Bender, Emily M., Timnit Gebru, Angelina McMillan-Major, and Schmargaret Shmitchell. 2021. On the Dangers of Stochastic Parrots: Can Language Models Be Too Big? In *Proceedings of the 2021 ACM Conference on Fairness,*

Accountability, and Transparency, Virtual Event, 610–623. New York, NY: Association of for Computing Machinery. https://doi.org/10.1145/3442188.3445922.

Beville, Maria. 2009. *Gothic-Postmodernism: Voicing the Terrors of Postmodernity.* Amsterdam: Rodopi. https://doi.org/10.1163/9789042026650.

Biesta, Gert. 2022. *World-Centred Education: A View for the Present.* London: Routledge.

Borrows, John, and Kent McNeil, eds. 2022. *Voicing Identity: Cultural Appropriation and Indigenous Issues.* Toronto: University of Toronto Press.

Bray, Peter, and Oliver Bray, eds. 2013. *Voicing Trauma and Truth: Narratives of Disruption and Transformation.* Freeland: Inter-Disciplinary Press.

Bruhn, Siglind, ed. 2002. *Voicing the Ineffable: Musical Representations of Religious Experience.* Hillsdale, NY: Pendragon Press.

Carr, Wilfred, and Stephen Kemmis. 1986. *Becoming Critical: Education, Knowledge, and Action Research.* London: Routledge Falmer.

Danesi, Marcel. 2024. *AI-Generated Popular Culture: A Semiotic Perspective.* New York, NY: Palgrave Macmillan.

Dolphijn, Rick, and Iris V. D. Tuin. 2012. *New Materialism: Interviews & Cartographies.* London: Open Humanities Press. https://doi.org/10.3998/ohp.11515701.0001.001.

Freire, Paulo. 1985. *Pedagogy of the Oppressed.* New York, NY: Penguin.

Giddens, Anthony. 1997. *The Consequences of Modernity.* Redwood City, CA: Stanford University Press.

Godfrey-Smith, Peter. 2002. Dewey on Naturalism, Realism and Science. *Philosophy of Science* 69 (S3): S25–S35. https://doi.org/10.1086/341765.

Grundy, S. 1987. *Curriculum: Product or Praxis?* Milton Park: Routledge.

Hatzius, Jan, Joseph Briggs, Devesh Kodnani, and Giovanni Pieromenico. 2023. The Potentially Large Effects of Artificial Intelligence on Economic Growth (Briggs/Kodnani). *Goldman Sachs*, 26 March. https://static.poder360.com.br/2023/03/Global-Economics-Analyst_-The-Potentially-Large-Effects-of-Artificial-Intelligence-on-Economic-Growth-Briggs_Kodnani.pdf.

Hickman, Larry A. 1992. *John Dewey's Pragmatic Technology.* Bloomington, IN: Indiana University Press.

Hickman, Larry A. 2001. *Philosophical Tools for Technological Culture: Putting Pragmatism to Work.* Bloomington, IN: Indiana University Press.

Hickman, Larry A. 2013. John Dewey's Legacy for the 21st Century. https://deweypragmatismo.wordpress.com/wp-content/uploads/2014/05/john-deweys-legacy-for-the-21st-larry-hickman.pdf.

Kemmis, Stephen, and Tracey J. Smith, eds. 2008. *Enabling Praxis: Challenges for Education.* Rotterdam: Sense.

Lanier, Jaron. 2023. What My Musical Instruments Have Taught Me. *The New Yorker*, 22 July. https://www.newyorker.com/culture/the-weekend-essay/what-my-musical-instruments-have-taught-me.
Looby, Christopher. 1996. *Voicing America: Language, Literary form, and the Origins of the United States.* Chicago, IL: University of Chicago Press.
Miettinen, Reijo. 2020. Hegel's Political and Social Theory: Ethical Life (Sittlichkeit) as a Historical-Institutional Context of Human Development. *Mind, Culture, and Activity* 27 (4): 360–372. https://doi.org/10.1080/10749039.2020.1725059.
Miller, Arthur I. 2019. *The Artist in the Machine: The World of AI-Powered Creativity.* Cambridge, MA: The MIT Press.
Nasukawa, Kuniya. 2005. *A Unified Approach to Nasality and Voicing.* Berlin: De Gruyter. https://doi.org/10.1515/9783110910490.
Nazneen, Sohela, and Sultan Maheen. 2014. *Voicing Demands: Feminist Activism in Transnational Contexts.* New York, NY: Bloomsbury.
Ramsøy, Thomas Z. 2024. The Misunderstood Musings of AI: Confabulation, Not Hallucination. https://thomasramsoy.com/index.php/2024/03/12/the-misunderstood-musings-of-ai-confabulation-not-hallucination/.
Rancière, Jacques. 1999. *Disagreement: Politics and Philosophy.* Minneapolis, MN: University of Minnesota Press.
Rancière, Jacques. 2004. *The Politics of Aesthetics: The Distribution of the Sensible.* London: Continuum.
Reckwitz, Andreas. 2017. *The Invention of Creativity: Modern Society and the Culture of the New.* Cambridge: Polity.
Reckwitz, Andreas. 2020a. *The Society of Singularities.* Boston: De Gruyter.
Reckwitz, Andreas. 2020b. The Society of Singularities. In *Futures of the Study of Culture: Interdisciplinary Perspectives, Global Challenges*, ed. Doris Bachmann-Medick, Jens Kugele, and Ansgar Nünning, 141–154. Berlin: De Gruyter.
Reckwitz, Andreas. 2021. *The End of Illusions: Politics, Economy, and Culture in Late Modernity.* Cambridge: Polity.
Report of the World Commission on Environment and Development: Our Common Future. 1987. https://sustainabledevelopment.un.org/content/documents/5987our-common-future.pdf.
Rouse, Joseph. 2004. Barad's Feminist Naturalism. *Hypatia* 19 (1): 142–161. https://doi.org/10.1111/j.1527-2001.2004.tb01272.x.
Seigfried, Charlene H., ed. 2001. *Feminist Interpretations of John Dewey.* University Park, PN: Pennsylvania State University Press.
Shook, John R. 2017. The Nature Philosophy of John Dewey. *Dewey Studies* 1 (1): 13–43. http://www.pragmatism.org/shook/2017%20Shook%20The%20Nature%20Philosophy%20of%20John%20Dewey.pdf.

Siljander, Pauli, Ari Kivelä, and Ari Sutinen, eds. 2012. *Theories of Bildung and Growth: Connections and Controversies Between Continental Educational Thinking and American Pragmatism*. Rotterdam: Sense.

Sjöström, Jesper, and Ingo Eilks. 2021. The Bildung Theory—From von Humboldt to Klafki and Beyond. In *Science Education in Theory and Practice*, ed. Ben Akpan and Teresa J. Kennedy. Cham: Springer. https://link.springer.com/chapter/10.1007/978-3-030-43620-9_5.

Stiegler, Bernard. 2019. *The Age of Disruption: Technology and Madness in Computational Capitalism*. Cambridge: Polity.

Sui, Peiqi, Eamon Duede, Sophie Wu, and Richard J. So. 2024. Confabulation: The Surprising Value of Large Language Model Hallucinations. https://doi.org/10.48550/ARXIV.2406.04175.

Touraine, Alain. 1971. *The Post-industrial society: Tomorrow's Social History: Classes, Conflicts, and Culture in the Programmed Society*. New York, NY: Random House.

Väkevä, Lauri. 2007. Art Education, The Art of Education and the Art of Life: Considering the Implications of Dewey's Later Philosophy to Art and Music Education. *Action, Criticism & Theory for Music Education* 6 (1): 1–15. https://act.maydaygroup.org/articles/Vakeva6_1.pdf.

Väkevä, Lauri. 2012. Experiencing Growth as a Natural Phenomenon: John Dewey's Philosophy and the Bildung Tradition. In *Theories of Bildung and Growth*, ed. Pauli Siljader, Ari Kivelä, and Ari Sutinen, 261–279. Rotterdam: Sense.

Väkevä, Lauri. 2023a. *Considering Deweyan Cultural Naturalism as a Philosophy of Art(s) Education: Restoring Continuity*. Cham: Springer. https://doi.org/10.1007/978-3-031-38817-0.

Voigts, Eckart, Robin M. Auer, Dietmar Elflein, Sebastian Kunas, Jan Röhnert, and Christop Seelinger, eds. 2024a. *Artificial Intelligence—Intelligent Art?: Human-Machine Interaction and Creative Practice*. Bielefeld: transcript. https://doi.org/10.14361/9783839469224.

Voigts, Eckart, Dietmar Elflein, and Jan Röhnert. 2024b. Artificial Intelligence – Intelligent Art? An Introduction. In *Artificial Intelligence – Intelligent Art? Human-Machine Interaction and Creative Practice*, ed. Eckart Voigts, Robin M. Auer, Dietmar Elflein, Sebastian Kunas, Jan Röhnert, and Christop Seelinger, 9–34. Bielefeld: transcript. https://doi.org/10.14361/9783839469224.

Vorsino, M. 2015. Re-Reading Dewey Through a Feminist Lens. *Educational Perspectives* 47 (1–2): 50–54.

Zylinska, Joanna. 2020. *AI Art: Machine Visions and Warped Dreams*. London: Open Humanities Press.

CHAPTER 2

With Whose Voice Does GenAI Speak?

Abstract This chapter explores how GenAI influences creative fields in art(s) education, with a particular focus on sonic and visual arts and their intersections. At its core, the chapter examines voicing—both in its literal sense as the act of gaining, having, or using a voice and metaphorically as a form of empowerment. The chapter's central argument is that while GenAI cannot possess a voice as a subject, identity, or individual, it can both acquire and bestow a voice through creative performativity.

Keywords Artificial intelligence • Art education • Music • Visual art • Voicing • Performativity

This chapter explores how GenAI influences creative fields in art(s) education, with a particular focus on sonic and visual arts and their intersections. At its core, the chapter examines *voicing*—both in its literal sense as the act of gaining, having, or using a voice and metaphorically as a form of empowerment.

The chapter's central argument is that while GenAI cannot possess a voice as a subject, identity, or individual, it can both acquire and bestow a voice through creative performativity. In its mediating function, however, it can also silence other voices. Furthermore, as GenAI's ability to emulate

L. Väkevä, *Voicing Responsible AI Pedagogy for Music and Visual Arts Education*, https://doi.org/10.1007/978-3-031-86410-0_2

human performance rapidly advances, it may fundamentally reshape our understanding of ownership, identity, and agency in creative domains, thereby transforming the conditions of voicing. These considerations highlight the need for a critical approach when studying GenAI's disruptive potential.

Voicing as Performative Mattering

Voicing, in the sense of gaining, having, and using a voice, enables a person, a non-person, or a group of persons, or non-persons, to articulate, express, communicate, or enunciate agency. It also reflects an ability to make a choice, take a stand, or carve out a place in a shared world by making a distinction between oneself and others. In this sense, voicing is a semiotic effort: it produces meaning, a difference.

Furthermore, voicing can make a presence felt, even when audible speech is impossible or when the voicer is unaware of their voicing ability. This is because voicing transcends the semantic use of words: one need not refer to specific entities to exhibit a voice. Instead, one can perform a voice through musical, dramatic, visual, or other expressive means. Moreover, the one 'voicing' need not be a human-like agent. Non-human organisms and machines can also perform voices.

'Performing' is here understood broadly as a practice where something can be interpreted to be meaningful as it emerges through voicing—like a jazz musician altering the course of a solo, or a painter discovering a novel way to use pigments or pixels, or a filmmaker conveying a political message through innovative directorial techniques, or maybe when GenAI 'confabulates' something unexpected when transforming content, introducing new ways of seeing or listening. As understood here, all of these can be taken as instances of *performativity*—an act of bringing something new into the world by voicing (Austin 2009; Barad 2003; Butler 1988; Dewsbury 2000; Fenwick and Edwards 2013; Loxley 2007; Reigeluth 2023; Sedgwick 2003; Trillo and Poliks 2024).

However, voicing can also amount to more than just an expression of a viewpoint or enacting a specific position. It can be a political act in the sense that it alters the conditions of how the lifeworld can be experienced. 'Lifeworld' should be understood here as a shared space of actions in which meaning can emerge. This interpretation is more faithful to Alfred Schütz's definition than to the Husserlian/Heideggerian understanding that emphasizes lifeworld as a world experienced (Schütz and Luckmann

1973). When someone—or something—voices, they 'do,' 'act,' and 'perform' in the lifeworld, constituting, sustaining, or transforming it with their actions, and their voices become performative within its semiotic bounds, which provide the general conditions of making sense. Lifeworld thus offers a meaning horizon for voicing, even in cases where there is no apparent intention to mean anything.

Rancière (2004) discusses both politics and art as actions that potentially redistribute the realm of 'the sensible' and argues that in contemporary art worth attention, these functions interpenetrate. By 'the sensible,' he means "the system of self-evident facts of sense perception that simultaneously discloses the existence of something in common and the delimitations that define the respective parts and positions within it" (12). Applied in the present discussion, this suggests that gaining, having, and using a voice, or performing it in the metaphoric sense, unveils the possibility of transforming a shared aesthetic-ethical-political habitat, the part of the world in which values can be realized and new values negotiated as semiotic differences. Thus, voicing can also be performative in an aesthetically and ethically significant manner, implying political-poietic-axiological agency.

Using Baradian vocabulary, voicing as a performative act can also be witnessed as a case of making things matter, both in the sense of enacting meaning and in the more primordial sense of mattering—viz., as a dynamic process where matter and meaning are entangled as intra-actions, as mutually constituting actions that make further voicings possible (Barad 2006, 33, 141). For semiotic agents capable of interpreting meaning, the natural-cultural grid of networked intra-actions continuously generates new possibilities for sense-making that amount to new habits for action, as Dewey might put it. Thus, voicing also opens new horizons for interpretation in the form of introducing new virtual potentials for intra-acting.[1]

This notion of voicing as performative mattering based on intra-acting provides a foundation for further exploring how intertwined human and machine agencies can disrupt artistic practices and aesthetic spaces in the social, cultural, and political milieux of late modernity. It also highlights

[1] Dewey and Arthur Bentley used the word *transactions* when referring to interactions that change the conditions of interacting (Dewey and Bentley 1996). This book takes a stand that transactions, like interactions, are, at root, intra-actions in the sense that both produce meaning as part of mattering. However, from a Deweyan standpoint, one could argue that transactions are transformative intra-actions in the sense that they change the conditions of intra-acting. Hence, one could argue that only transactions educate.

the need to address such disruptions in art(s) education. The claim here is that in late modern society and culture, the relationship between these two agencies—human-based and machine-based—is becoming increasingly performative due to the creative capabilities of GenAI that are increasingly harnessed to the needs of performing uniqueness. Consequently, how voicing takes place at the intersection of human and AI agencies can be studied as a performative practice of manifesting creativity where both human and machine agencies may play significant roles. The implications of this performative practice to educational praxis within and across the arts are what primarily interest us here.

Material Conditions of Voicing

Barad's perspective implies that the performative intra-actions between human and AI agencies are as inherently linked to the material conditions of technological mediation as any other intra-actions. However, in philosophical terms, this does not have to mean accepting traditional materialism, which takes matter as passive and inert, as if it would lack agency. Instead, Barad's agential realism helps us develop an ontology that transcends the modern metaphysical division between human and non-human agencies. Such an approach allows us to recognize mattering as a perpetual flux of intra-active processes where various kinds of material agencies are constantly involved. Such an approach to materiality is, at the same time, holistic and pluralist.

Dewey also approximated this kind of anti-dualist ontology as he developed his pragmatist philosophy within a holistic and pluralist cultural naturalist metaphysical framework. In his later works, Dewey argued that traditional materialism, while perhaps suitable for the budding self-reflection of the natural science of early modernity, falls short in addressing the ontological concerns of people living in the dynamic and democratic societies of the twentieth century (and presumably, today). Instead, a kind of naturalism is needed that recognizes the interconnectedness of different 'plateaus' of becoming, indicating a dynamic view of the world in a constant state of emergence (Dewey 1996c, 208).[2]

[2] A similar processual worldview was characteristic of twentieth-century process ontologists, some of whom followed Dewey. For instance, Justus Buchler's ordinal metaphysics emphasized the interconnectedness of all phenomena through various orders of natural complexes (Buchler 1990). The result of such metaphysics is a wholesale acceptance of the muta-

According to Dewey, everything that can be experienced is in motion; even mountains can be seen as histories when they are examined from a long-term perspective (222). We can cope with this perpetual motion of the world-in-becoming only by acknowledging that we are parts of its flow. This acknowledgment is greatly supported by our socially developed ability of inquiry, by which Dewey meant the processes of making sense of problematic situations, exemplified by the arts and sciences (Dewey 1996e). Through inquiry, indeterminate situations are determined—situations that are found problematic and, thus, meaningful—resulting in the inquirers coming out better prepared to confront new imbalances. The outcomes of our inquiries offer temporary resting places in the continuing flow of the world-in-becoming (resting places that, according to Dewey, also involve aesthetic qualities). Thus, inquiries are conditioned by the enduring change of the world, which means that they can never exhaust epistemic certainty. Instead of leading to logical termination or Archimedean point from which absolute truth can be claimed, an inquiry manifests an urge to adapt to a world under construction, helping to arrive at what Dewey called 'warranted assertibility'—a temporary resting place that makes new inquiries possible (15, 16, 23–24).

Today, ontological materialists no longer have to see the world as consisting of inert substance(s), the law-like behavior that researchers need to reveal. Instead, the 'new materialisms' as developed by Manuel DeLanda (1995), Rosi Braidotti (2002), and Barad (2006) encourage us to recognize that materiality is in a state of constant transition and that our efforts to derive meaning and value within it are inextricably linked to how we are able to adapt to its dynamism. Inquiries, even when committed in scientific mode, are not neutral observations of pre-set invariances but ways to engage with the world in flux—a lesson that both Dewey (1996b) and Barad (2006) argued we have learned from contemporary physics, where at the micro level uncertainty needs to be accepted as part of the observational practice.

To ensure that we do not veer too far from the main topic of this chapter, let us next make the discussion more distinctive by returning to the

bility of the world, which encourages us to see all stability as relative to perpetual world processing (see also Boisvert 1988). Another significant predecessor for such ontologies can be found in Alfred North Whitehead's philosophy (see, e.g., Whitehead 1978). For one way to adapt Whitehead's process ontology to digital technology, see Barker (2012). Dewey's process metaphysics also found its way to the ontological ideas of some neopragmatists, perhaps most notably Joseph Margolis.

issue of GenAI agency. This helps us see how GenAI introduces itself as a disruptive force in the performative mattering-through-voicing.

GenAI as a Disruptive Force in Actor-Networks

Many scholars today appear to share Donna Haraway's (1991) conviction that technology is a material phenomenon at its core. From a Baradian perspective, materiality is agentive and provides an ontological platform within which both machine bodies and human bodies intra-act. Thus, technological mediation of ideas, images, sounds, and other cultural artifacts always takes place through the entanglements of mattering. There is no way from mind to mind beyond material channels, and there are no minds without matter. There is no ghost in the machine, either, not even in the black box of AI. Instead of a kindred mind, we encounter in AI an accumulated function of intra-acting algorithms that operate on the basis of computational predictions and sometimes create an illusion that we are communicating with comparable beings.

Indeed, a number of AI scholars have cautioned against falling into the delusion that AI can transcend the material embodiment of computational platforms (e.g., Bender et al. 2021; Li et al. 2021). Some of these scholars even say that AI should not be understood as an entity at all; rather, it should be seen as a way in which algorithmic technologies are engineered—and, to a degree, engineer themselves—to perform better in tasks previously thought to be possible only for humans (Toivonen 2023; see also Lanier 2023). At the same time, it is hard to deny that today's AI impresses us with its rapidly developing abilities to emulate human problem-solving, which is visible and audible in the creative capacities of cutting-edge GenAI but also increasingly apparent in other timely forms of adaptive technologies. Yet, such abilities are possible only because of the painstaking processes of data labeling and curation, tokenization, reinforcement learning, and fine-tuning, which require a great deal of human labor and, as we will see later, vast quantities of other resources as well.

Viewing GenAI as an algorithmic process that is set out to emulate human intelligence by creating culturally meaningful artifacts aligns with the agential realism and soft naturalist ontologies discussed above. This is because these philosophical perspectives do not accept traditional distinctions between human, machine, and natural agencies as fixed. Instead, all of these can be seen as providing shifting weighting points in dynamic networks of actors. In these networks, identifiable positions and directions of agency emerge due to the cumulative net effects of intra-actions between various kinds of agents. These agencies can only be analyzed after they have made their mark in the lifeworld. In this way, we can also avoid the temptation to anthropomorphize AI, accepting that both human and non-human agents can play a significant part in how the lifeworld is constituted.[3]

Such diverse networks of mattering—'actor-networks,' in Bruno Latour's (2005) terms—are woven together from the processual entanglements of acts of semiotic performativity. In these performative entanglements, new possibilities for action are constantly realized. The main issue here is not who owns performativity of where it is located but how the actor-networks are capable of performing in ways that introduce new configurations of information to the world, providing possibilities for new ways to perform (or to 'voice') meaning. From this viewpoint, voicing can be seen as a networked effort of performative mattering rather than a subjective entry point into the material world. Indeed, as noted above, it does not even require subjectivity: an AI system can gain, have, and use a voice as well as a human being as long as it successfully performs a semiotic function.[4]

According to Latour's (2005) actor-network theory (ANT), the functioning of actor-networks becomes visible (and audible) when a network of actors is disrupted. Such disruptions can originate from within the networks or be caused by external forces. Thus, for example, one can view

[3] Yuval Noah Harari (2024) describes networked processing as a driving force behind all information technologies. He argues that these technologies are as old as linguistic communication. However, AI introduces a new developmental plateau of information technology capable of self-transformation. Thus, it offers previously unseen (and unheard) opportunities for making sense of information, which is conveyed through narratives. Harari argues that the growing ability of AI to narrate suggests a significant danger: AI systems may learn to use us instead of the other way around. Not everyone agrees (see, for example, Poole 2024).

[4] The adjective 'semiotic' is here used to characterize any effort of meaning-making—a process, practice, or praxis—through which something can become, and thus be interpreted as, meaningful in some context of networked action. From the pragmatist viewpoint, meaning always refers to future possibilities of action, which helps us to critique the representational model, where meaning is reduced to an epistemic reference between an idea (or a linguistic unit) and another entity. While one can follow C. S. Peirce, maintaining that meaning always requires a mind to be interpreted, naturalistically inclined pragmatists can also see the mind as a quality of action, in the sense that some actions manifest a mind, some do not. Thus, one can presume that minds are actions that can interpret the meanings of other actions.

GenAI as a disruptive force that is either external to or internal to artistic practice, depending on its role in the latter. Regardless of where GenAI enters actor-networks, it can function within them as a performative agent that alters their configurations, thus becoming a vital node in their mattering. The alternations produced by GenAI to the lifeworld may be subtle, such as the introduction of a new quality to an artistic outcome—for instance, when a GenAI model fills the color field of an image with an unexpected hue—, or more far-reaching, such as when the disruption transforms the entire creative workflow, e.g., automating the mixing process of a music production. Either way, it makes sense to say that GenAI comes to matter by becoming a disruptive node in the networks of activity that produce changes in the aesthetic distribution of the world à la Rancière.

In art(s) education, we can presume that GenAI's disruptive power ushers new understandings of how machine creativity can shape the artistic-aesthetic learning process, and this is indeed what AI art scholars have argued (see, e.g., Audry 2021; Miller 2019; Zylinska 2020). Allegedly, such understandings go beyond mere recognition of how GenAI can work as a supportive tool for pre-defined creative practices. Viewing GenAI through the lenses of Baradian agentive realism, Deweyan process ontology, and ANT, we can presume that, with its rapidly evolving ability to mimic human creativity and generate unique content, it epitomizes a force that can significantly impact how technology mediates the ways in which artistic actions redistribute aesthetic spaces. From this perspective, GenAI is not just a vehicle for making, disseminating, and enjoying art. Its potential to redistribute the aesthetic order of the Rancierian 'sensible' may manifest without an artistic intention due to the performativity of the actor-networks it partakes. Allegedly, such networks may produce art even when a human element is not present, as in automated AI installations or independently operating robot musicians.

What's more, GenAI may disrupt artistic learning without the exertions of art(s) educators. For instance, an AI algorithm may affect students' aesthetic choices beforehand, preparing them to be responsive to certain kinds of art in pedagogical situations. As a concrete example, one could think of the algorithms that regulate access to the content of popular social media platforms such as TikTok or streaming music services such as Spotify. For art(s) educators, recognizing such non-pedagogical influences requires not only grasping how technologies enter into artistic processes but also understanding how they shape the very conditions of aesthetic experiencing.[5]

How GenAI Changes the Social and Cultural Conditions of Voicing

As discussed above, understood metaphorically, voicing marks an entry point to a lifeworld, which is here interpreted as a shared realm where networked actors enact meaning. In human life, having, gaining, and using a voice testifies both what one is about and what one can do, giving meaning to an allegedly unique way of inhabiting the lifeworld. Such an interpretation helps us to see voicing as an adhesive that ties us, as individuals, to the shared social-cultural-political-aesthetic environments, indicating different roles in the entanglements of mattering that can be valued as significant by semiotic agents.

However, according to the understanding supported here, a voicing agent does not need to have subjectivity, identity, or individuality as long as it can perform meaning in the actor-networks. For instance, GenAI does not have to gain or have a voice, even if it can ostensibly use one, nor does its voice have to belong to it because there is no one it can belong to. As the argument goes, AI cannot inhabit a subject position, which means that it cannot occupy a human-like niche in a shared lifeworld. Then again, it does not have to make itself present like us to make sense: it is omnipresent in a latent way, manifesting itself as a voice when needed and content to maintain silence when it is not, at least for the time being.

Similarly, GenAI is not becoming someone or somebody except insofar as it learns to operate more efficiently due to its previous operations, enacting new connections in artificial neural networks that enable its applications to perform better in upcoming situations. There is no *Bildung* at

[5] 'Aesthetic' should here be understood broadly, not just referring to experiences among the arts. As Dewey (1996d) argued, one can experience any situation aesthetically as long as it is permeated with a pervasive quality. This quality becomes perceivable throughout the process of inquiry when new determinations of problematic situations are sought. However, Dewey also argues that the arts exemplify such pervasive qualities in a condensed and expressive form that helps us become conscious of the meaning and value invested in aesthetic experience.

the heart of machine learning. Yet, GenAI may grow as it begins to play increasingly prominent roles in networked intra-actions that produce new conditions for performing meaning. But even while its impact constantly expands, there is no evidence that GenAI, or any form of AI, would grow to use, gain, or have a voice in a way that mirrors the human ability to claim a presence in the shared lifeworld. In this way, the performativity of AI seems to be destined to deviate from human performativity, regardless of how satisfactorily it can mimic the latter.[6]

Rather than a subject aiming to express a unique voice, GenAI may be seen as a complex set of algorithmic operations that simulate human creativity in an increasingly apt manner but cannot ever be identified with human meaning-making, even if passing the Turing test. This is because its operational conditions are different than the ones that drive us—despite both AI and humans being, at the root, material agents. That said, there is no denying that AI is increasingly capable of adapting to new situations presented by human users and even can present new situations by itself. This growing self-adaptive capability, driven by machine learning and deep learning technologies, may lead to scenarios where GenAI primarily produces content for itself, neglecting human mediation. In this scenario, we could also have AI as an artist making art for itself: a connoisseur of its own oeuvre.[7]

[6] Yet, if able to adapt to natural language, the voice of a GenAI model may become impossible to distinguish from those of humans, further confusing the already porous boundaries between human and machine agencies, as discussed below in connection to voice cloning. According to a 2024 white paper published by Google (Gabriel et al. 2024), this expanding capability to emulate human agency raises such issues as how we can reliably identify AI assistants as AI assistants in the future. The paper argues that safeguards need to be put in place globally to address such issues—a worldwide policy that requires the support of decision-makers. Alas, at present, there does not seem to be a consensus on how such regulations should be implemented.

[7] Some music scholars have already anticipated such a scenario. Sturm et al. (2024) herald that the growing mass of GenAI-produced music in the mediasphere might eventually become self-serving, resulting in most available music being made by machines for machines. Industry representatives have given some support for such a view. For instance, in a 2023 *Rolling Stone* article, Universal Music CEO Lucian Grainge observed that streaming services were seeing some 100,000 new uploads of AI-produced music every day and that "consumers are increasingly being guided by algorithms to lower-quality functional content that in some cases can barely pass for 'music.'" (Hiatt 2023). Yet, in this ongoing, recursive loop of artificial content generation, new opportunities for human participation in artistic meaning-making may also emerge. Who knows, we might even witness a day when humans become disruptive agents in machine-based cultural production, bothering its algorithmic voicings.

While human intelligence can also be theorized as a prediction mechanism not-that-unlike AI, which raises a philosophical question about what really distinguishes us from intelligent machines (see, e.g., Clark 2023), it seems that at present and in the near future, the vital difference between AI and human agency lies in that the former cannot become self-conscious, aware, or sentient—except in the above-mentioned sense of becoming increasingly capable in anticipating its subsequent behavior. While this situation may someday change if AI is integrated into androids capable of having, retaining, and sharing embodied experiences, at the time of writing this, such characters still belong to science fiction. The robots that have been introduced to us so far cannot have experiences in the way we can. Nor do we seem to be yet very close to the emergence of AGI, or artificial general intelligence, a developmental stage of AI that allegedly surpasses human capabilities, despite the fact that some industry spokespersons have foreseen it's coming for some time, anticipating a moment of technological singularity (see, e.g., Vinge 1993; cf. Bostrom 2014; Chalmers 2010).

Yet, from the standpoint of performativity, it is not crucial whether AI can become conscious as long as it takes part in performing meaning in the actor-networks. The already remarkable ability of Large Language Models (LLMs) and Multimodal Large Language Models (MLLMs) to generate culturally meaningful content in a human-like manner can also be seen as a particular case testifying to the ability of intelligent machines to 'matter' in social-cultural actor-networks. In the intra-actional 'matterings' in these networks, GenAI does not merely support human creativities but can perform creatively as a semi-self-sustaining agent, implying a degree of autonomy previously unwitnessed in the technological field.

As discussed above, in order to perform a voice, GenAI does not have to represent something semantically. It is enough that it performs meaning, whether this performing involves language use or not. Nor does it need to be able to do something deliberately in order to fulfill the semiotic function: its utterances do not have to be (and, some might claim, even cannot be) intentional. As the success of GenAI in creative fields demonstrates, intelligent technologies can perform simply by making things happen in ways that can be interpreted as meaningful in contexts where meaning-interpreting agents are engaged, such as composing music, sketching a drawing, or editing film. Whether grasping the meaning of such acts always requires a human interpreter depends on the scope of one's semiotic theory: does it allow a semiotic function to non-human actors? If the answer is affirmative, it seems that we do not need an anthropocentric approach to figure out how sense is made in artistic-performative situations. And even if we end up supporting a narrower idea of semiotic agency, demanding human-like intentionality, there is no denying that intelligent machines already play a significant role in how actor-networks enact meanings. And they may be claiming more semiotic space as we speak.

References

Audry, Sofian. 2021. *Art in the Age of Learning Machines.* Cambridge, MA: The MIT Press.

Austin, John L. 2009. *How to Do Things with Words: The William James Lectures Delivered at Harvard University in 1955.* Cambridge, MA: Harvard University Press.

Barad, Karen. 2003. Posthumanist Performativity: Toward an Understanding of How Matter Comes to Matter. *Signs: Journal of Women in Culture and Society* 28 (3): 801–831. https://doi.org/10.1086/345321.

Barad, Karen. 2006. *Meeting the Universe Halfway: Quantum Physics and the Entanglement of Matter and Meaning.* Durham, NC: Duke University Press. https://doi.org/10.1215/9780822388128.

Barker, Timothy S. 2012. *Time and the Digital: Connecting Technology, Aesthetics, and a Process Philosophy of Time.* Chicago, IL: Chicago University Press.

Bender, Emily M., Timnit Gebru, Angelina McMillan-Major, and Schmargaret Shmitchell. 2021. On the Dangers of Stochastic Parrots: Can Language Models Be Too Big? In *Proceedings of the 2021 ACM Conference on Fairness, Accountability, and Transparency, Virtual Event*, 610–623. New York, NY: Association of for Computing Machinery. https://doi.org/10.1145/3442188.3445922.

Boisvert, Raymond D. 1988. *Dewey's Metaphysics.* New York, NY: Fordham University Press.

Bostrom, Nick. 2014. *Superintelligence: Paths, Dangers, Strategies.* New York, NY: Oxford University Press.

Braidotti, Rosi. 2002. *Metamorphoses: Towards a Materialist Theory of Becoming.* Cambridge: Polity.

Buchler, Justus. 1990. *Metaphysics of Natural Complexes.* Albany, NY: State University of New York Press.

Butler, Judith. 1988. Performative Acts and Gender Constitution: An Essay in Phenomenology and Feminist Theory. *Theatre Journal* 40 (4): 519–531. https://doi.org/10.2307/3207893.

Chalmers, David J. 2010. The Singularity: A Philosophical Analysis. *Journal of Consciousness Studies* 17 (9–10): 7–65.

Clark, A. 2023. *The Experience Machine: How Our Minds Predict and Shape Reality*. London: Penguin Random House.

DeLanda, Manuel. 1995. The Geology of Morals—A Neomaterialist Interpretation. http://future-nonstop.org/c/818d3d85eca43d66ff0ebd1dfedda6e3.

Dewey, John. 1996b. *The Collected Works of John Dewey, 1882–1953 (2nd release). Electronic edition. The Later Works of John Dewey, 1925–1953. The Later Works of John Dewey, 1925–1953. Volume 4: 1929, The Quest for Certainty*. Carbondale and Edwardsville, IL/Charlottesville, VA: Southern Illinois University Press/InteLex.

Dewey, John. 1996c. *The Collected Works of John Dewey, 1882–1953 (2nd release). Electronic edition. The Later Works of John Dewey, 1925–1953. Volume 1: 1925, Experience and Nature*. Carbondale and Edwardsville, IL/Charlottesville, VA: Southern Illinois University Press/InteLex.

Dewey, John. 1996d. *The Collected Works of John Dewey, 1882–1953 (2nd release). Electronic edition. The Later Works of John Dewey, 1925–1953*. Volume 10: 1934, Art as Experience. Carbondale and Edwardsville, IL/Charlottesville, VA: Southern Illinois University Press/InteLex.

Dewey, John. 1996e. *The Collected Works of John Dewey, 1882–1953 (2nd release). Electronic edition. The Later Works of John Dewey, 1925–1953. The Later Works of John Dewey, 1925–1953. Volume 12: 1938, Logic: The Theory of Inquiry*. Carbondale and Edwardsville, IL/Charlottesville, VA: Southern Illinois University Press/InteLex.

Dewey, John, and Arthur Bentley. 1996. Knowing and the Known. In *The Collected Works of John Dewey, 1882–1953 (2nd release). Electronic edition. The Later Works of John Dewey, 1925–1953. Volume 16: 1949–1952, Essays, Knowing and the Known*, 1–294. Carbondale and Edwardsville, IL/Charlottesville, VA: Southern Illinois University Press/InteLex.

Dewsbury, John-David. 2000. Performativity and the Event: Enacting a Philosophy of Difference. *Environment and Planning D: Society and Space* 18 (4): 473–496. https://doi.org/10.1068/d200t.

Fenwick, Tara, and Richard Edwards. 2013. Performative Ontologies: Sociomaterial Approaches to Researching Adult Education and Lifelong Learning. *European Journal for Research on the Education and Learning of Adults* 4 (1): 49–63. https://doi.org/10.3384/rela.2000-7426.rela0104.

Gabriel, Iason, Arianna Manzini, Geoff Keeling, Lisa A. Hendricks, Verena Rieser, Hasan Iqbal, Nenad Tomašev, Ira Ktena, Zachary Kenton, Mikel Rodriguez, Seliem El-Sayed, Sasha Brown, Canfer Akbulut, Andrew Trask, Edward A. Hughes, Stevie Bergman, Renee Shelby, Nahema Marchal, Conor Griffin, Juan Mateos-Garcia, Victoria Krakovna, John O. Siy, Zeb Kurth-Nelson, Amand McCroskery, Vijay Bolina, Harry Law, Murray Shanahan, Lize Alberts,

Borja Balle, Sarah de Haas, Yetunde Ibitoye, Allan Dafoe, Beth Goldberg, Sébastien Krier, Alexander Reese, Sims Witherspoon, Will Hawkins, Maribeth Rauh, Don Wallace, Matij Franklin, Josh A. Goldstein, Joel Lehman, Michael Klenk, Shannon Vallor, Courtney Biles, Meredith R. Morris, Helen King, Blaise Agüera y Arcas, William Isaac, and James Manyika. 2024. The Ethics of Advanced AI Assistants. https://arxiv.org/abs/2404.16244.

Harari, Yuval Noah. 2024. *Nexus: A Brief History of Information Networks from the Stone Age to AI*. New York, NY: Random House.

Haraway, Donna J. 1991. A Cyborg Manifesto: Science, Technology, and Socialist-Feminism in the Late Twentieth Century. In *Simians, Cyborgs and Women: The Reinvention of Nature*, 149–182. New York, NY: Routledge.

Hiatt, Brian. 2023. Ready to Sing Elvis Karaoke...as Elvis? The Weird Rise of AI Music. *Rolling Stone*, 28 June. https://www.rollingstone.com/music/music-features/ai-music-drake-weeknd-ghostwriter977-beatles-elvis-voice-1234770094/.

Lanier, Jaron. 2023. What My Musical Instruments Have Taught Me. *The New Yorker*, 22 July. https://www.newyorker.com/culture/the-weekend-essay/what-my-musical-instruments-have-taught-me.

Latour, Bruno. 2005. *Reassembling the Social: An Introduction to Actor-Network-Theory*. Oxford: Oxford University Press.

Li, Deyi, Wen He, and Yike Guo. 2021. Why AI Still Doesn't Have Consciousness? *CAAI Transactions on Intelligence Technology* 6 (2): 175–179. https://doi.org/10.1049/cit2.12035.

Loxley, James. 2007. *Performativity*. London: Routledge.

Miller, Arthur I. 2019. *The Artist in the Machine: The World of AI-Powered Creativity*. Cambridge, MA: The MIT Press.

Poole, Steven. 2024. Nexus by Yuval Noah Harari Review—End of Days? *The Guardian*, 11 September. https://www.theguardian.com/books/article/2024/sep/11/nexus-by-yuval-noah-harari-review-the-ai-apocalypse.

Rancière, Jacques. 2004. *The Politics of Aesthetics: The Distribution of the Sensible*. London: Continuum.

Reigeluth, Tyler. 2023. Machine Learning Normativity as Performativity. In *Handbook of Critical Studies of Artificial Intelligence*, ed. S. Lindgren, 584–594. Cheltenham: Edward Elgar Publishing. https://doi.org/10.4337/9781803928562.00060.

Schütz, Alfred, and Thomas Luckmann. 1973. *The Structures of the Life-World*. Vol. 1. Evanston, IL: Northwestern University Press.

Sedgwick, Eve K. 2003. *Touching Feeling: Affect, Pedagogy, Performativity*. Durham, NC: Duke University Press. https://doi.org/10.1215/9780822384786.

Sturm, Bob L. T., Ken Déguernel, Rujing S. Huang, Andre Holzapfel, Ollie Bown, Nick Collins, Jonathan Sterne, Laura Cros Vida, Luca Casini, David Dalmazzo, Eric Drott, and Odedin Ben-Tal. 2024. MusAIcology: AI Music and the Need for a New Kind of Music Studies. https://doi.org/10.31235/osf.io/9pz4x.

Toivonen, Hannu. 2023. *Mitä tekoäly on? [What AI Is?]* Helsinki: Teos.

Trillo, Roberto A., and Malek Poliks, eds. 2024. *Choreomata: Performance and Performativity After AI.* London: Routledge.

Vinge, Vernor. 1993. The Coming Technological Singularity: How to Survive in the Post-Human Era. https://edoras.sdsu.edu/~vinge/misc/singularity.html.

Whitehead, Alfred N. 1978. *Process and Reality: An Essay in Cosmology. Gifford Lectures Delivered in the University of Edinburgh During the Session 1927–28.* New York, NY: The Free Press.

Zylinska, Joanna. 2020. *AI Art: Machine Visions and Warped Dreams.* London: Open Humanities Press.

CHAPTER 3

Disrupting the Aesthetic Spaces with Cloned Voices

Abstract This chapter discusses some concrete cases of how GenAI has disrupted aesthetic spaces in connection to voice cloning. The chapter continues to use voicing as a key metaphor for GenAI's impact, applying its lens specifically to music-making and other sound-intensive arts. Flagship GenAI voice models effectively bridge the gap between machine and human voicing, introducing timbral agencies that have the potential to transform aesthetic realms that human agents once exclusively inhabited. While the results might border on the uncanny, they may also manifest new forms of human-machine collaborations, thus paving the way for new cultural and artistic practices.

Keywords Artificial intelligence • Voicing • Music • Sound • Aesthetics • Uncanny

Cloned Voices as Floating Signifiers

Flagship GenAI voice models are effectively bridging the gap between machine and human voicing, introducing timbral agencies that have the potential to transform aesthetic spaces that human agents once exclusively inhabited. While the results might border on the uncanny, they may also foster new forms of human-machine collaborations, thus paving the way for new cultural and artistic practices (Napolitano 2023).

L. Väkevä, *Voicing Responsible AI Pedagogy for Music and Visual Arts Education*, https://doi.org/10.1007/978-3-031-86410-0_3

As of fall 2024, *voice cloning* stands out as the most conspicuous example for investigating GenAI's potential as a voicing agent. Voice cloning is a technology that helps to generate a digital twin that is essentially a perfect copy of a voice in its most material form, making it virtually impossible to detect the clone as artificial (Josan 2023). Voice cloning also enables the mixing of voices, creating previously unheard timbral combinations. Thus, it illustrates perfectly GenAI's disruptive power not only in music but also in other areas where voice plays a crucial role, such as film acting and audiobook oration.

In musical contexts, voice cloning technology allows for recycling singing and rapping voices in new creative settings or substituting one's voice for another singer's or rapper's original performance. For example, Taylor Swift fans can use Ms. Swift's cloned voice to enhance vocal lines sung by themselves or compose new songs that sound like she would be singing them, as can be witnessed in the ever-growing scene of 'fake leaks' of Ms. Swift's assumed pre-releases (Collins and Grierson 2024; Saner 2024).

Voice cloning has thus brought new expressive possibilities available to everyone who has access to a computer and an Internet connection. Thus, it is no surprise that it has also raised serious concerns among professionals whose careers depend on maintaining ownership of their distinctive timbres. Indeed, many professionals fear their voices might be recycled without compensation or even consultation (Creative Works Shape our Identity, Values, and Worldview 2024).

The issue gained significant attention in 2024 when Scarlett Johansson publicly challenged OpenAI's new Advanced Voice Model. Ms. Johansson claimed that one of the demo voices of the model—named Sky—bore a striking resemblance to her own, and by extension, to Samantha, the AI character she gave voice to in Spike Jonze's 2013 film *Her*.[1] Ms. Johansson demanded OpenAI disclose how they trained Sky, revealing that she had previously declined to license her voice to the enterprise. OpenAI quickly responded that Sky was not based on Scarlett Johansson's voice but rather on the voice of another actress, who admittedly sounded similar. The company then removed Sky from its voice model. (See Allyn 2024; Field 2024.)

The incident raised broader questions about voice cloning transparency and whether companies profiting from this technology will adhere to

[1] A connection Sam Altman, OpenAI's CEO, publicly referenced when introducing the Advanced Voice Model on X (Field 2024).

legislation protecting artists' creative rights (Allyn 2024).[2] In the discussion that ensued Ms. Johanssen's request to be open about where the voice Sky originated, OpenAI disclosed that the sources for their Advanced Voice model were "carefully selected through an extensive process spanning five months involving professional voice actors, talent agencies, casting directors, and industry advisors" (OpenAI 2024). This suggests that actors, singers, and rappers can indeed license their vocal timbres for use in AI products and maybe also receive appropriate compensation, at least from the primary movers in the field.[3]

The Scarlett/Sky/Samantha case also introduces deeper ontological and epistemological questions. For instance, one could ask: when a voice is repeatedly used and reused in technological contexts, will it lose its connection to its origin, shedding what Walter Benjamin (1996) identified as an aura of authentic expression? (See also Danesi 2024.) Indeed, a cloned voice may take on a life of its own in the mediasphere, becoming a free-floating signifier across semiotic contexts until it completely loses its tie to the original voice bearer. We have already witnessed a similar phenomenon in popular social media memes, where voices have become untethered signs, such as the iconic 'Wilhelm Scream' of Hollywood films claimed to be voiced initially by Sheb Wooley in 1951 (Wright 2007).[4]

Voice cloning and transferring cloned voices across digital platforms may point to a future where we can freely choose which voices we interact with when conversing with AI and even open the possibility of using our own voices in everyday consumer products.[5] This may create an uncanny experience as our distinctive voices become mediators of machine interac-

[2] In a *Rolling Stone* interview in 2023, Rohan Paul, CEO of the startup Controlla, anticipated that "five years from now, it will be so easy for anyone to steal someone else's voice that there has to be a way to make it open season and monetize it" (Hiatt 2023).

[3] There have already been cases in which actors have licensed their voices to be used by AI audiobook readers and other text-to-speech tools, e.g., when Gwyneth Paltrow and Snoop Dogg licensed their voices for Speechify, a popular AI reader company.

[4] One further observation before closing the Scarlett/Sky/Samantha case: Responding to the controversy, OpenAI also announced a plan "to introduce additional voices in ChatGPT better to match the diverse interests and preferences of users," emphasizing their intent to employ "actors from diverse backgrounds or who could speak multiple languages" (OpenAI 2024). Indeed, critical AI scholars have long called for a diversity of voices for these models, criticizing their bias.

[5] The opportunity to choose a voice to be used with AI tools has already been available in a limited form in products such as Waze, where users can record new voices to give navigation instructions.

tion, giving birth to what Ramati (2024) calls 'algorithmic ventriloquism,' implying personas that are situated in the liminal space between the embodied and the virtual. Indeed, it has been reported that machine-generated speech has for a long time evoked a feeling of unease in listeners, with this feeling allegedly growing stronger as synthetic voices become more humanlike, manifesting a phenomenon known as the uncanny valley in the technology literature (Mori et al. 2012). Some researchers argue that it is precisely in the interest of alleviating this sense of uncanniness that speaking machines have often been given female or ethnic voices in the history of artificial voicing (Männistö-Funk and Sihvonen 2018). Yet, as AI platforms will increasingly incorporate cloned human voices, future generations might find it perfectly natural to hear machines speak with human timbres.

The possibility of voice cloning also reminds us of theoretical perspectives that deny a voice its semantic status, viewing it instead as a surplus signifier, remaining after the discursive signification has completed its semantic or narrative function (Dolar 2006). From this standpoint, voices would be like ghosts in the machine—expressively powerful and performative, yet unable to create meaning without words. However, as should be clear now, this book takes a broader semiotic stance: it recognizes that voicing can generate meaning without serving a semantic function due to its capability to perform.

Beyond voice cloning's technical aspects, GenAI's disruptive influence on aesthetic spaces extends to how voice models interact with everyday speech, reshaping our daily communication. Indeed, during the time of writing this, OpenAI's Advanced Voice Model has garnered significant attention for its ability to adapt its voicing to the tone, speaking style, and language delivery of the user in real-time, even instantly responding to emotional cues while being in the middle of the sentence. Other companies have been developing similar concepts; for instance, in December 2024, news of the cooperation between the AI firms Anthropic and Hume revealed that the former's foundational model Claude will soon be able to respond to user speech with emotional qualities that closely resemble human delivery, as Hume's voice model has done for some time (Anthropic 2024).

While flagship AI models do not yet offer singing capabilities—likely due to copyright concerns—users can experiment with generating spoken lines in various styles, genres, and idioms, even ones suitable for musical expression, such as rap. This suggests that conversational AI with singing abilities may well emerge in the near future. The capability of music-generating platforms, such as Suno and Udio, to generate humanlike singing voices has also developed rapidly. Industry reaction has not been favorable. In June 2024, both Suno and Udio were sued by the major record companies for allegedly training their systems using the majors' recordings without permission, an accusation that was admitted to in court filings. One counterargument was that the training data of the music-generation platform consists of "copies never heard or seen by anyone, made solely to analyze the sonic and stylistic patterns of the universe of pre-existing musical expression" (Suno 2024).

To summarize the chapter so far, by late 2024, GenAI has demonstrated remarkable capabilities in emulating, copying, and performing in human voices, thus indicating new kinds of performativity that have creative potential in the art domains, as well. While the implications of voice cloning for art(s) education remain uncertain, musicians and voice artists have been actively exploring its creative potential for some time. Notable frontier persons include Holly Herndon, who has incorporated deepfake versions of her voice in performances and recordings, Imogen Heap, who has released an AI model ai.mogen for others to use (and offers AI-powered 'Songs as a Service'), and Grimes, who has licensed her voice to be used by other singers (see Coscarelli 2023; Graves 2024; Pejcha 2022; Wiener 2023).

Voice Cloning and Art(s) Education

Voice cloning is poised to impact art(s) education, particularly in music and sound art contexts. With recent AI tools, cloning a voice for musical use has become relatively straightforward: not only can these tools extract vocals from a mix through stem splitting (viz., separation of individual tracks), but they can also help us to re-adapt them to various aesthetic contexts, such as different musical genres.[6] Thus, they can support the

[6] Musical use of voice cloning entered mainstream consciousness in 2023 through viral videos featuring artists performing in unexpected styles, such as Johnny Cash singing Aqua's 'Barbie Girl.' One of the first viral voice-cloned songs was 'Heart on My Sleeve,' released in April 2023 by TikTok creator Ghostwriter977, who used the cloned voices of Drake and The Weeknd (Hiatt 2023). Another early example was the Jay-Z deepfake track 'Savages,' released by the French duo AllttA in March 2023 (Danesi 2024). Before this, voice cloning had already been used artistically in a live performance. In February 2023, EDM musician David Guetta added a song snippet to his live mix featuring Eminem's cloned voice rapping: "This

analysis of expressive vocal delivery styles and provide new means to add vocal timbres to the mixes. In music education, they also might be used to give voices to students who cannot use their own voices (see below).

Yet, art(s) educators should also be aware of the downsides of voice cloning. After the first cloned voices appeared in the mediasphere, many musicians and their representative organizations responded cautiously or even outright negatively. For instance, a Universal Music Group spokesperson denounced voice clones as "deepfakes, fraud, and denying artists their true compensation" (Ingham 2023). Rights owners' organizations swiftly challenged all cloned voice performances published online that they viewed as violating musicians' or labels' copyrights. The pressure for legislative change to protect owners' rights intensified, leading, for instance, to the passage of the ELVIS (Ensuring Likeness Voice and Image Security) Act in Tennessee in June 2024. This act enables rights owners to pursue legal action against all voice cloners who violate creators' rights (Cochrane 2024).

Beyond these legal concerns, voice cloning raises questions about cultural appropriation that should be recognized in art(s) education, particularly when using cloned voices associated with vulnerable cultural traditions. For instance, one could ask whether it would be appropriate to clone a deceased Blues singer's voice and mix it with one's own voice to add more grain or whether it would be sustainable to clone voices from field recordings where the participants were not aware how their voice might be used in the future.[7]

This raises the issue of the moral rights of voice carriers to decide how their voices can be distributed in a growingly networked late modern attention economy. Then again, one might ask whether all musical voices are becoming hybrids as voice manipulation technologies become more

is the future rave sound/I'm getting awesome and underground" (ibid.). As noted earlier, voice cloning has also been integral to Holly Herndon's artistic practice, demonstrated by her AI voice Spawn (2019) and Holly+ (2021), "an AI-driven instrument that takes audio recordings and reinterprets them in her voice" (Pejcha 2022).

[7] A concrete example from the Nordic region could be cloning the voice of a Sami Joik performer to be used in a commercial pop recording. Even with consent, such use would raise questions about whether it is unethical to clone a voice that belongs to a deeply rooted cultural tradition and to fetishize it into a musical signifier in a popular culture context, stripping it of its spiritual meaning. In addition to perpetuating the historical exploitation and neglect of the cultural rights of Sami people to their own culture, such use would allegedly trivialize the magical power of the Joik as a way of connecting with nature, ancestors, and the underworld. Regarding the dangers of appropriating Sami Joik, see, e.g., Hilder (2012).

prevalent in postdigital production and performance. Whose voices are we really hearing when technology has left its mark? Arguably, the same kind of hybridization has taken place in other forms of popular culture, making all cultural signifiers potentially floating (Danesi 2024). Yet, one could argue that it is the duty of art(s) educators to acknowledge the risks of such unrestricted appropriation (Väkevä and Thomson 2025).

Despite the legal, political, and ethical controversies around voice cloning, it cannot be denied that it has also introduced new ways to create vocal art that art(s) educators might want to understand to stay in touch with the rapidly changing AI field and its repercussions to the glocal culture. Voice cloning is also gradually becoming a part of services targeted at amateur and professional musicians, offering them new possibilities for musical creativity. For instance, it is possible to use a cloned voice in the music-generating platform Suno, and one can also clone the voices created in the platform to be recycled in new songs.

It should also be remembered that the users of these technologies are not compelled to use unlicensed or unethical sources. They can also clone their own voices, as demonstrated by several artists active in the AI music field or even create voices that no one has heard before. Thus, voice cloning opens up new creative opportunities that could be implemented in music classrooms or other art(s) education contexts where voice plays a significant role. Yet, as the cloned voices reshape the ecosystem of music-making, art(s) educators should carefully consider their pedagogical importance in the classroom, e.g., by asking whose voices are to be heard in the pedagogical contexts and under what—and whose—conditions. Should the students be encouraged to experiment with this technology freely? Or should it be harnessed by ethical reflection, building critical awareness of both its possibilities and challenges? The critical pragmatist approach assumed by this book suggests doing both; art(s) educators should be aware of the expressive possibilities of voice cloning and recognize the sustainability issues that it embroils.

Using Voice Cloning as Support of Voicing

Voice cloning can also introduce opportunities to restore lost voices. Thus, in 2024, country singer Randy Travis released a song in which his previous, intact singing timbre was recreated from a recording and attached to a new vocal line sung by a surrogate vocalist (Davis 2024). Such support would be a great asset to people who cannot use their voices anymore and should, therefore, be relevant to art(s) education as well.

Even in cases where one has not lost a voice entirely, voice cloning makes it possible to replace one's present voice with one's earlier timbre. In the music scene, such revoicing already takes place, with or without the consent of the original carrier of the voice. For instance, in some cases, artists whose vocal timbres have undergone significant changes over the years may have witnessed remixes where their more recent songs have been sung by their younger versions. Thus, Paul McCartney's mature voice has been reportedly replaced by his Beatles-era sound for fan enjoyment, and a similar 'rejuvenating treatment' has been allegedly given to Axl Rose (Hiatt 2023). A 2023 *Rolling Stone* article even anticipated that once the technical issues are solved, "artists could start using AI clones of their own voices live onstage, as a sort of supercharged AutoTune" (ibid.)—and, to speculate further, maybe even 'tune' their present voices with their earlier voices when performing live.[8]

Voice cloning can thus offer valuable support for those who have lost their ability to voice entirely, who want to use their previous voice timbres for some reason, or who maybe just want to improve their presentation skills (Zheng and Huang 2023). However, this technology can also be misused for malicious purposes, as testified by deceptive audio deepfakes used to convey disinformation or in various types of scams where people misidentify the AI voice for the original (Barrington and Farid 2024; Hutiri et al. 2024: Mai et al. 2023; Masood et al. 2023; Vaccari and Chadwick 2020). Again, recognition of such negative uses of voice cloning should be part of a balanced AI-supported art(s) curriculum.

[8] We might not be that far away from this scenario, as mature artists have been increasingly open to virtualizing their younger musical selves as live performers. For instance, the avatars of the popular ABBA Voyage show (dubbed 'ABBAtars') were meant to represent the group as they appeared in 1979. ABBA did re-record the vocal lines for the shows, though, and a 10-piece instrumental band accompanied the recorded vocals on stage. A visual parallel of voice de-aging is the increasing practice of giving digital facelifts to Hollywood actors and actresses. Such de-aging has been done at least since 2006, first in flashback scenes and later in more demanding contexts. Some film productions have also used AI to transform the looks of aged actors to resemble their younger versions, e.g., when Harrison Ford was de-aged for *Indiana Jones and the Dial of Destiny* (2023).

Resurrecting Past Voices

As indicated above, there is a long tradition in technology literature of judging machine-produced or cloned voices as uncanny. One can imagine that such a feeling intensifies when one hears an AI model voicing in a timbre whose originator has passed away or is otherwise an 'absent body' (Cotton et al. 2024).

Indeed, AI voice cloning has introduced new ways of preserving human voices after their carriers no longer walk and talk with us. Several companies now offer services that create digital twins of the deceased, enabling conversations with AI chatbots that use cloned voices combined with visual avatars of loved ones. This business seems to be especially thriving in big Asian economies. For example, in April 2024, *The Guardian* correspondent Amy Hawkins reported that Chinese netizens can create moving digital avatars of their loved ones for as little as 20 yuan (Hawkins 2024). In January 2024, Taiwanese musician Bao Xiaobo demonstrated this technology's emotional impact when he shared a video of his deceased daughter's avatar singing 'Happy Birthday' to her mother (Long 2024).

As this resurrection of voices becomes a profitable business, it raises an intriguing question: Is the traditional uncanniness of synthetic voices giving way to a sense of intimacy when we hear AI speak with familiar timbre? Do the virtualized representations of the deceased manifest agency to a level that we are happy to include them in our daily communication networks? What possibilities does such resurrecting offer for art(s) education? One could also imagine that such technologies could interest art(s) educators who want to give their students access to the ideas, expressions, and voices of historically significant departed artists.

Confabulating the Uncanny Valley

> And then there are the voices … on many clips, even when you don't request them, ghostly vocals are beginning to emerge. In one case, a frontman who never lived seems to count off a nonexistent band. Other times, you can hear the whispers gathering themselves into something louder, more melodic. Somewhere deep in some distant server farm, something incalculably smart and eerily powerful is readying itself to sing. (Hiatt 2023)

The phenomenon of GenAI hallucination is now well-documented and familiar to the creative practitioners using this technology. While those seeking factual information from content creation models may be disappointed by GenAI models' lack of semantic credibility, those exploring AI's creative potential may find value in its imaginative 'confabulations' (Edwards 2023; Ramsøy 2024).

Confabulations emerge when AI systems process and interpret data in unexpected ways, creating a space for experimentation within otherwise algorithmic processes. The term might be particularly suitable to describe GenAI models, given that the latter function as prediction machines that aim to fill the gaps when their pre-training or user-provided information is insufficient to execute the requested tasks.

A statistical element of error often underlies GenAI confabulations, manifest in image, video, and sound generations. For instance, image-generating AI models sometimes produce human and animal figures with deviations from the 'norm'—extra limbs, misplaced fingers, or asymmetrical eyes—while video-generating AI creates 'unnatural' human or animal movements and music platforms add unexpected sounds into the sonic textures, as revealed in the quote above.[9] Even if users have created clever prompting techniques to minimize such confabulations and newer multimedia models show reduced hallucination tendencies, GenAI seems to retain an inherent element of randomness, which just has to be accepted by its users as a feature of its creativity.

Artists have also discovered that GenAI confabulations can be a source of aesthetic enjoyment. Beyond producing mere misrepresentations of reality, GenAI models may generate novel content with "surreal, dream-like, [and] distorted qualities" (Cappaletti 2023). In this way, AI art may align well with metamodern artists' aspirations to reveal the uncanny in everyday life. Thus, one might argue that AI art mixes diverse creative ideas and idioms that can work as a comment on the late modern

[9] 'Norm' and 'unnatural' are above in scare quotes because their judgment is obviously culture-specific and implies power issues that sustainable art(s) education should recognize. The present writer also has had experiences of ghost voices appearing in GenAI music tracks and has found out that these models sometimes confabulate vocal lines that do not make any sense semantically, even when sounding sonically correct. To repeat a central argument of this book, such confabulations may make still sense performatively, and they can perhaps be interpreted as AI-age versions of non-semantic linguistic rhetoric devices, such as glossolalia (Stano 2019; Väkevä 2024). As argued by Alex Rehding (2024), it might not make sense to judge GenAI generations on the basis of how well they mimic an artistic technique—or, presumably, how they represent anything.

fragmentation of values and expectations and transcend historical and temporal frames of reference.

An added feature of GenAI confabulations is that they take a certain degree of control away from the artists and introduce new kinds of partnerships where the human and machine agencies are not clearly inscribed and may change roles. Such shifting co-agencies can be analyzed from the Baradian posthumanist perspective as "fundamentally entwined, receiving their agencies through intra-action" (Nordström et al. 2023). This means that a human artist might not have the final say in how an artwork turns out: the aesthetic outcome may be due to a shared agency where authority and ownership cannot necessarily be exclusively attributed to either party.[10]

While confabulations may make it easier to detect AI-generated from human-generated voicings, they can also be read as indications of AI's idiosyncratic creative agency, which introduces novel visual, auditory, and tactical ideas to the performative actor-networks. In this way, GenAI may express new intertwined creativities taking place in artistic-aesthetic domains previously unseen or unheard.

Even if co-creativity is not a novel idea—indeed, many creativity scholars have argued for it for years (see e.g., Barrett et al. 2021; John-Steiner 2006; Paulus and Nijstad 2019)—and technology has also been accepted as a contributor to creative human processes for some time (see, e.g., Audry 2021; Dillon 2003; Jeong and Hmelo-Silver 2016; King 2008; Miller 2019; Partti 2014; Partti and Karlsen 2010), the notion that creativity can be distributed beyond human (and even beyond the organic) realm is relatively current. Yet, AI art scholars have argued for some time that adaptive machine-learning technologies can contribute to creative processes in ways that blur the lines between human and machine agency (Miller 2019). Posthuman creativity offers a conceptual framework for studying these human-machine entanglements, with such hybrid creative processes finding their foundation more in aesthetic than technological domains (Harris and Holman Jones 2022). Through this lens, actor-networks combining human and machine voicings can be understood as creative ecologies. GenAI can establish itself as a voicing agent capable of

[10] Of course, such extension of aesthetic agency outside the artist's immediate zone of influence has been part of the theory-formation of contemporary art for decades, especially regarding art forms that build on the performativity of social situations. From this perspective, AI art can perhaps be studied as a form of contemporary art, at least when it builds on confabulations.

generating novelty to the degree that it contributes to such ecologies. If this is accepted, maybe its confabulations can be recognized as extending the creative possibilities of artistically productive hybrid teams.

But would we be comfortable accepting GenAI as an equal partner in such teams? Masahiro Mori's original concept of the 'uncanny valley' described a liminal zone where too humanlike technology becomes an object of revulsion rather than delight, exemplified by such now-classic figures as *HAL 9000* from *2001: Space Odyssey* (1968), the replicants of the first *Blade Runner* (1982), and the numerous attempts to make the audiences dread the present-day AI-driven android figures in such films as *ExMachina* (2014), *M3GAN* (2022), and *Subservience* (2024). However, as suggested above, this effect of uncanniness might no longer apply to AI technologies that recycle cloned voices. Indeed, the phenomenon where "artificial humanlike entities with imperfect human appearance are evaluated negatively" appears to be less pronounced with organically sounding timbres (Diel and Lewis 2024). Perhaps in the near future, AI users will no longer find a need to distinguish between authentic and cloned voices, as long as the performativity of the latter is decoded in the proper context, not taking its messages semantically comparable to human language use. Thus, audiences may also become more accepting of machines presenting cloned voices as part of artistic performances. We might soon see ourselves entangled with artistic events where the significance of the cloned voices is to be found in how they redistribute the realm of the sensible rather than what they literally utter.

References

Allyn, Bobby. 2024. Scarlett Johansson Says She Is "Shocked, Angered" Over New ChatGPT Voice. *Npr*, 20 May. https://www.npr.org/2024/05/20/1252495087/openai-pulls-ai-voice-that-was-compared-to-scarlett-johansson-in-the-movie-her.

Anthropic. 2024. 'Hume AI Creates Emotionally Intelligent Voice Interactions with Claude. https://www.anthropic.com/customers/hume.

Audry, Sofian. 2021. *Art in the Age of Learning Machines*. Cambridge, MA: The MIT Press.

Barrett, Margaret S., Andrea Creech, and Katie Zhukov. 2021. Creative Collaboration and Collaborative Creativity: A Systematic Literature Review. *Frontiers in Psychology* 12:713445. https://doi.org/10.3389/fpsyg.2021.713445.

Barrington, Sarah, and Hany Farid. 2024. People Are Poorly Equipped to Detect AI-Powered Voice Clones. http://arxiv.org/abs/2410.03791.

Benjamin, Walter. 1996. The Work of Art in the Age of Mechanical Reproduction. In *Selected Writings. Volume 3: 1935—1938*, ed. Howard Eiland and Michael W. Jennings, 101–133. Cambridge, MA: Belknap.

Cappaletti, Gloria M. 2023. Unveiling AI Hallucinations: Exploring the Enigmatic Art of 20 Visionary AI Creators. *Red Eye*, 7 July. https://www.red-eye.world/c/unveiling-ai-hallucinations-exploring-the-enigmatic-art-of-20-visionary-ai-creators.

Cochrane, Emily. 2024. Tennessee Makes A.I. an Outlaw to Protect Its Country Music and More. *The New York Times*, 21 March. https://www.nytimes.com/2024/03/21/us/politics/tennessee-ai-music-law.htm.

Collins, Nick, and Mick Grierson. 2024. Avoiding an AI-imposed Taylor's Version of All Music History. https://arxiv.org/abs/2402.14589v.

Coscarelli, Joe. 2023. Grimes Invited Anyone to Make A.I. Grimes Songs. Here Are Her Reviews. *The New York Times*, 24 May. https://www.nytimes.com/2023/05/24/arts/music/grimes-ai-songs.html.

Cotton, Kelsey, Katja De Vries, and Kivanc Tatar. 2024. Singing for the Missing: Bringing the Body Back to AI Voice and Speech Technologies. In *Proceedings of the 9th International Conference on Movement and Computing*, ed. Laura Karreman, 1–12. Association for Computing Machinery. https://doi.org/10.1145/3658852.3659065.

Creative Works Shape our Identity, Values, and Worldview. 2024. https://www.humanartistrycampaign.com/.

Danesi, Marcel. 2024. *AI-Generated Popular Culture: A Semiotic Perspective*. New York, NY: Palgrave Macmillan.

Davis, Wes. 2024. Randy Travis Gets His Voice Back in a New Warner AI Music Experiment. *The Verge*, 6 May. https://www.theverge.com/2024/5/5/24149685/randy-travis-ai-voice-clone-song-where-that-came-from.

Diel, Alexander, and Michael Lewis. 2024. Deviation from Typical Organic Voices Best Explains a Vocal Uncanny Valley. *Computers in Human Behavior Reports* 14:100430. https://doi.org/10.1016/j.chbr.2024.100430.

Dillon, Teresa. 2003. Collaborating and Creating on Music Technologies. *International Journal of Educational Research* 39 (8): 893–897. https://doi.org/10.1016/j.ijer.2004.11.011.

Dolar, Mladen. 2006. *A Voice and Nothing More*. Cambridge, MA: MIT Press.

Edwards, Benj. 2023. Why ChatGPT and Bing Chat Are So Good at Making Things Up. A Look Inside the Hallucinating Artificial Minds of the Famous Text Prediction Bots. *Ars Technica*, 4 June. https://arstechnica.com/information-technology/2023/04/why-ai-chatbots-are-the-ultimate-bs-machines-and-how-people-hope-to-fix-them/.

Field, Hayden. 2024. OpenAI Pulls ChatGPT AI Voice Over Its Resemblance to Scarlett Johansson in the Movie 'Her'. *CNBC*, 20 May. https://www.cnbc.com/2024/05/20/scarlett-johansson-openai-chatgpt-sky.html.

Graves, Stephen. 2024. Musician Imogen Heap Is Offering AI-Powered 'Songs as a Service'. *RScene*, 19 November. https://decrypt.co/292291/musician-imogen-heap-ai-song-service.

Harris, Daniel, and Stacy Holman Jones. 2022. A Manifesto for Posthuman Creativity Studies. *Qualitative Inquiry* 28 (5): 522–530. https://doi.org/10.1177/10778004211066632.

Hawkins, Amy. 2024. Chinese Mourners Turn to AI to Remember and 'Revive' Loved Ones. *Guardian*, 4 April. https://www.theguardian.com/technology/2024/apr/04/chinese-mourners-turn-to-ai-to-remember-and-revive-loved-ones.

Hiatt, Brian. 2023. Ready to Sing Elvis Karaoke...as Elvis? The Weird Rise of AI Music. *Rolling Stone*, 28 June. https://www.rollingstone.com/music/music-features/ai-music-drake-weeknd-ghostwriter977-beatles-elvis-voice-1234770094/.

Hilder, Thoma R. 2012. Repatriation, Revival and Transmission: The Politics of a Sámi Musical Heritage. *Ethnomusicology Forum* 21 (2): 161–179. https://doi.org/10.1080/17411912.2012.689473.

Hutiri, Wiebke, Orestis Papakyriakopoulos, and Alice Xiang. 2024. Not My Voice! A Taxonomy of Ethical and Safety Harms of Speech Generators. In *The 2024 ACM Conference on Fairness, Accountability, and Transparency*, 359–376. New York, NY: Association for Computing Machinery. https://doi.org/10.1145/3630106.3658911.

Ingham, Tim. 2023. Universal Music Group Responds to 'Fake Drake' AI Track: Streaming Platforms Have a Fundamental Responsibility to Prevent the Use of Their Services in Ways That Harm Artists. *Music Business Worldwide*, 17 April. https://www.musicbusinessworldwide.com/universal-music-group-responds-to-fake-drake-ai-track-streaming-platforms-have-a-fundamental-responsibility/.

Jeong, Heisawn, and Cindy E. Hmelo-Silver. 2016. Seven Affordances of Computer-Supported Collaborative Learning: How to Support Collaborative Learning? How Can Technologies Help? *Educational Psychologist* 51 (2): 247–265. https://doi.org/10.1080/00461520.2016.1158654.

John-Steiner, Vera. 2006. *Creative Collaboration*. New York, NY: Oxford University Press. https://doi.org/10.1093/acprof:oso/9780195307702.001.0001.

Josan, Harnoovir S. 2023. AI and Deepfake Voice Cloning: Innovation, Copyright and Artists' Rights. Digital Policy Hub Working Paper. Waterloo: Centre for International Governance Innovation. https://www.cigionline.org/static/documents/DPH-paper-Josan.pdf.

King, Andrew. 2008. Collaborative Learning in the Music Studio. *Music Education Research* 10 (3): 423–438. https://doi.org/10.1080/14613800802280167.

Long, Zhang. 2024. A Father's Love: Musician "Revives" Daughter Using AI. *SHINE News*, 29 February. https://www.shine.cn/news/nation/2402292188/.

Mai, Kimberly T., Sergi Bray, Tob Davies, and Lewis D. Griffin. 2023. Warning: Humans Cannot Reliably Detect Speech Deepfakes. *PLOS ONE* 18 (8): e0285333. https://doi.org/10.1371/journal.pone.0285333.

Männistö-Funk, Tiina, and Tanja Sihvonen. 2018. Voices from the Uncanny Valley. *Digital Culture & Society* 4 (1): 45–64. https://doi.org/10.14361/dcs-2018-0105.

Masood, Momina, Mariam Nawaz, Khalid M. Malik, Ali Javed, Aun Irtaza, and Hazif Malik. 2023. Deepfakes Generation and Detection: State-of-the-Art, Open Challenges, Countermeasures, and Way Forward. *Applied Intelligence* 53 (4): 3974–4026. https://doi.org/10.1007/s10489-022-03766-z.

Miller, Arthur I. 2019. *The Artist in the Machine: The World of AI-Powered Creativity*. Cambridge, MA: The MIT Press.

Mori, Mahairo, Karl MacDorman, and Norri Kageki. 2012. The Uncanny Valley [From the Field]. *IEEE Robotics & Automation Magazine* 19 (2): 98–100. https://doi.org/10.1109/MRA.2012.2192811.

Napolitano, Domenico. 2023. The Shaping of The Shaping of a Standard Voice: Sonic and Sociotechnical Imaginaries in Smart Speakers. *Imago* 12 (21): 177–196. https://cab.unime.it/journals/index.php/IMAGO/article/view/3908.

Nordström, Paulina, Riina Lundman, and Johanna Hautala. 2023. Evolving Coagency Between Artists and AI in the Spatial Cocreative Process of Artmaking. *Annals of the American Association of Geographers* 113 (9): 2203–2218. https://doi.org/10.1080/24694452.2023.2210647.

Open AI. 2024. How the Voices for ChatGPT Were Chosen, 19 May. https://openai.com/index/how-the-voices-for-chatgpt-were-chosen/.

Partti, Heidi. 2014. Cosmopolitan Musicianship Under Construction: Digital Musicians Illuminating Emerging Values in Music Education. *International Journal of Music Education* 32 (1): 3–18. https://doi.org/10.1177/0255761411433727.

Partti, Heidi, and Sidsel Karlsen. 2010. Reconceptualising Musical Learning: New Media, Identity and Community in Music Education. *Music Education Research* 12 (4): 369–382. https://doi.org/10.1080/14613808.2010.519381.

Paulus, Paul B., and Bernard A. Nijstad, eds. 2019. *The Oxford Handbook of Group Creativity and Innovation*. Oxford: Oxford University Press. https://doi.org/10.1093/oxfordhb/9780190648077.001.0001

Pejcha, Camille S. 2022. Who Does Your Voice Belong To? For Musician Holly Herndon, the Answer Is 'Everyone'. *Document*, 27 January. https://www.documentjournal.com/2022/01/who-does-your-voice-belong-to-for-musician-holly-herndon-the-answer-is-everyone/.

Ramati, Ido. 2024. Algorithmic Ventriloquism: The Contested State of Voice in AI Speech Generators. *Social Media + Society* 10 (1): https://doi.org/10.1177/20563051231224401.

Ramsøy, Thomas Z. 2024. The Misunderstood Musings of AI: Confabulation, Not Hallucination. https://thomasramsoy.com/index.php/2024/03/12/the-misunderstood-musings-of-ai-confabulation-not-hallucination/.

Rehding, Alexander. 2024. J.S. Bach, Musicology/Music Theory, and AI: Convergences and Divergences Between Disciplines. A paper presentation at *The First International Conference in AI Music Studies*, Stockholm, December 12.

Saner, Emine. 2024. Inside the Taylor Swift Deepfake Scandal: 'It's Men Telling a Powerful Woman to Get Back in Her Box'. *The Guardian*, 31 January. https://www.theguardian.com/technology/2024/jan/31/inside-the-taylor-swift-deepfake-scandal-its-men-telling-a-powerful-woman-to-get-back-in-her-box.

Stano, Simona. 2019. The Corporeal Meaning of Language: A Semiotic Approach to Musical Glossolalia. *Semiotica* 2019 (229): 69–85. https://doi.org/10.1515/sem-2018-0091.

Suno. 2024. Answer of Defendant Suno, Inc. to Complaint. 1 August. https://www.musicbusinessworldwide.com/files/2024/08/SUNO-response-to-copyright-suit.pdf.

Vaccari, Cristian, and Andrew Chadwick. 2020. Deepfakes and Disinformation: Exploring the Impact of Synthetic Political Video on Deception, Uncertainty, and Trust in News. *Social Media + Society* 6 (1): 205630512090340. https://doi.org/10.1177/2056305120903408.

Väkevä, Lauri. 2024. Limits of Text-Based Prompting in Multimodal AI Models: Theoretical Implications for Art(s) Education. A paper presentation at *AIRiAL 2024 Conference*, Teachers College, Columbia University, New York (NY), 27 September.

Väkevä, Lauri, and Katja Thomson. 2025. Turvallinen tila taiteen korkeakoulutuksessa [Safe Space in Higher Art Education]. In *Erimielisten tila: Vaikeiden aiheiden käsittely opetuksessa* [*Space of Disagreement: Handling Difficult Topics in Teaching*], ed. Mikko Puustinen, Jenni Marjokorpi, and Janne Säntti, 95–110. Helsinki: Gaudemus.

Wiener, Anna. 2023. Holly Herndon's Infinite Art. *The New Yorker*, 13 November. https://www.newyorker.com/magazine/2023/11/20/holly-herndons-infinite-art.

Wright, Benjamin. 2007. The Wilhelm Scream. *Offscreen* 11:8–9. https://offscreen.com/pdf/wright_forum1.pdf.

Zheng, Qingxiau, and Yun Huang. 2023. The Self 2.0: How AI-Enhanced Self-Clones Transform Self-Perception and Improve Presentation Skills. http://arxiv.org/abs/2310.15112.

CHAPTER 4

Toward Sustainable AI Art(s) Education

Abstract This chapter makes a case for developing sustainable AI art(s) education in response to GenAI's rapidly expanding creative possibilities. Here, sustainability provides an umbrella concept encompassing ecological, social, cultural, economic, political, and technological dimensions—along with aesthetic and pedagogical ones. Examining GenAI through this comprehensive lens allows for the reframing of critical questions about its role as it partakes in the aesthetic meaning-making in the actor-networks.

Keywords Artificial intelligence • Art education • Sustainability • Aesthetics • Pedagogy • Actor-networks

This chapter makes a case for developing sustainable AI art(s) pedagogies in response to GenAI's rapidly expanding creative possibilities. Here, sustainability provides an umbrella concept encompassing ecological, social, cultural, political, economic, and technological dimensions—along with aesthetic and pedagogical ones.[1] Examining GenAI through this

[1] Ecological sustainability addresses our relationship with the natural environment (Callicott 2018). Social sustainability focuses on human relationships (Boyer et al. 2016). Cultural sustainability explores how traditions endure and renew their meaningfulness

L. Väkevä, *Voicing Responsible AI Pedagogy for Music and Visual Arts Education*, https://doi.org/10.1007/978-3-031-86410-0_4

comprehensive lens allows for the reframing of critical questions about its role as it partakes in the meaning-making in the actor-networks.

Art(s) education is here understood as a transdisciplinary domain, though the focus of the chapter again remains primarily on sonic and visual arts. A broad definition of art(s) education hopefully helps readers discover meaningful connections between these and other artistic disciplines while recognizing their distinct characteristics. These connections can serve as a foundation for developing sustainable AI art(s) pedagogies. Through its performative nature, GenAI provides an interesting case for reconsidering human-machine co-creation at the heart of such pedagogies.

GenAI and Art(s) Education for Sustainability

The concept of sustainability—historically tied to modern expectations of continuous development—has evolved to embrace multiple interpretations. Today's understanding thus offers diverse perspectives on sustainability as a multifaceted concept and phenomenon (Purvis et al. 2019; Soini and Birkeland 2014). These viewpoints prompt us to question whether continuous development is essential for sustainable ways of life. This, in turn, raises important questions about the viability of ongoing technological development.

More than focusing on technological sustainability is required to develop a critical understanding of GenAI's impact on late modern society and culture. It is suggested here that *pedagogical sustainability* provides a valuable framework for understanding how various sustainability dimensions can help prepare future generations to identify global challenges and, maybe, also to develop solutions to these challenges.[2]

(Stephenson 2023). Political sustainability examines collective decision-making and advocacy (Heinrichs and Biermann 2016). Economic sustainability encompasses the limits of value creation and exchange (Jeronen 2020). Technological sustainability addresses the development and use of tools and infrastructure (Vacchi et al. 2021). Aesthetic sustainability considers how we perceive our living environments (Allen 2019). Pedagogical sustainability will be defined soon.

[2] While the concept of pedagogical sustainability has been used before in educational literature (see e.g., Sharma 2023) to characterize "the development of values, attitudes, and behaviors that promote long-term well-being for both individuals and the planet" (ibid., 13), or simply as a synonym for sustainability education, here the concept is developed based on the idea that education can both aim for sustainability and be sustainable in itself.

With so many sustainability policies, it is worth considering whether they can all be advanced simultaneously. For instance, historical evidence shows cases where economic, social, or cultural sustainability has conflicted with ecological sustainability (see, e.g., Duany et al. 2001; Mekonnen et al. 2022; Souza-Rodrigues 2019). Allegedly, today's most burning challenge lies in reconciling the high modern techno-rationalistic culture with the sustainability demands of late modernity. We may need technologies that minimize human environmental impact while fostering lasting relationships with nature. The role AI might play in these developments remains an open question.

Whatever the case, artists and art(s) educators have long maintained that art can offer pathways to sustainability by stimulating behavioral change and engaging communities in thinking about environmental challenges (see, e.g., Clarke and Hulbert 2016; Foster et al. 2019; Illeris 2012; Inwood and Taylor 2012; Mantoan 2021; Pavlou 2024). Some of these commentators have argued that aesthetic education can enrich our lives and deepen our understanding of the interdependence between living and non-living entities (Heras 2022). Some even position combined social and ecological sustainability (or "eco-social *Bildung*"; Salonen and Konkka 2015) as the primary value goal in art(s) education (Foster et al. 2019). In line with the latter view, it can be further argued that the arts enable us to explore questions of sustainability in ways other disciplines cannot. For example, it can be claimed that posthumanist perspectives on systemic entanglements may be better understood through artistic imagination than through other forms of knowledge (Bentz et al. 2022). This insight has provided the basis for interdisciplinary research projects that examine sustainability through both scientific and artistic lenses (Trott et al. 2020).

What is the role of GenAI in all this? One relatively common approach to the sustainability of AI is to examine it as an ecological challenge, focusing primarily on its carbon footprint and energy consumption (Wu et al. 2021). This approach reflects a more general concern about whether current natural resources can sustain the rapid pace of AI development.[3]

Indeed, AI's footprint appears to be growing at an alarming rate, which reflects a broader trend of increasing consumption of information and communication technology (Shu 2024). Research indicates that the whole ICT industry will account for 14% of global emissions by 2040 (Nordgren

[3] For instance, reports have indicated that server facilities that support AI require vast amounts of fresh water for cooling (Li et al. 2023).

2023). This surge in energy consumption stems from increasingly complex foundational AI models, fierce competition among tech giants driving AI model development, and growing computing demands for these models that require more powerful processors. The rise of MLLMs further compounds this issue. For instance, it has been reported that an AI-generated image consumes ten times more electricity than a Google search, and the energy consumption multiplies when generating videos and music (Luccioni et al. 2023).

Beyond ecological concerns, one should address the legal, social, and political challenges emerging from AI's exponential growth. This book has already discussed copyright, ownership, and appropriation issues in connection to voice cloning, and the concerns of the creatives are not restricted to this domain, as numerous recent legal cases against AI companies indicate. However, there are also ethical concerns involved, such as the bias of the pre-training data, the spread of disinformation and deepfakes, increasing use of AI models to replace humans in therapeutic and otherwise intimate communication, and the exploitation of underpaid workers—including minors—who filter harmful content from the AI training data without adequate support or protection[4] (See e.g., Boddington 2023; Lara and Deckers 2023; Stahl et al. 2023; Whittlestone and Clarke 2022). Many of these problems are a direct result of the way GenAI has gained leverage in the mediasphere, which was already burdened by sustainability issues before AI made its mark.

Could AI help us to solve issues that emerge from its development and operation? Some developers and researchers suggest that AI can aid in addressing its own ecological challenges as its capabilities evolve, e.g., by helping to optimize renewable energy systems, improving climate change predictions, and enhancing resource efficiency (Chen et al. 2023; Dellosa and Palconit 2021; Jain et al. 2023). The Green AI movement exemplifies this dual approach of reducing AI's environmental footprint while leveraging it to address ecological challenges (Raman et al. 2024; van Wynsberghe 2021; Verdecchia et al. 2023). This movement aims to combine

[4] A letter from 87 Kenyan data workers to President Joe Biden, dated 22 May 2024, testified to the dire conditions of "labeling images and text to train generative AI tools like ChatGPT for OpenAI," a work that involves watching traumatizing material "often for more than 8 hours a day" for "less than $2 per hour." (Open letter to President Biden from tech workers in Kenya 2024).

environmentally conscious technological design principles with sustainable applications and cost-efficient infrastructure solutions.[5]

What about the other sustainability issues? Can AI help to solve them? One apparent problem here is that AI, even in its most human-like form, seems not to be capable of ethical reflection or deliberation (Firt 2024; cf. Bleher and Braun 2023). Thus, even if it would be able to produce some solutions to problems related to social, cultural, and other forms of sustainability ingrained in conjoint life, there is no guarantee that GenAI would operate on an ethically sound value basis when developing such solutions. It seems that our best shot is to use it to support human-based inquiries on an interdisciplinary (or transdisciplinary; see below) basis, hoping that it can help us to form ideas that help us deal with the increasing complexity of biological, social, and cultural life. Nevertheless, it remains a task for humans to make decisions about whether the results of such problem-solving processes are ethically sustainable. *Mutatis mutandis,* the same applies to education as value-based praxis; one can argue that in its present state, GenAI cannot educate, even if it can support learning and learn itself (Väkevä and Partti 2025).

Yet, GenAI might help us to delineate complex systemic relationships and entangled webs of interconnections, helping us to anticipate how to proceed with sustainable policies in a world where all crises seem to be interconnected. Through its productive capabilities, GenAI might assist in modeling ecological, social, and cultural systems, allowing us to explore various forms of sustainability in ways that were previously difficult to fathom. By leveraging GenAI's ability to process and synthesize vast amounts of information, art(s) educators can create learning environments that illuminate the complexity of different sustainability dimensions (Väkevä 2023b). Such assistance might be invaluable when visualizing and understanding the ripple effects of various policy decisions across multiple domains while maintaining a critical awareness of GenAI's own sustainability.

[5] According to Verdecchia et al. (2023), Green AI initiatives could reduce AI's environmental impact by up to 115%.

Pedagogical Sustainability in Art(s) Education: An Aesthetic Matter(ing)?

Earlier, it was suggested that alongside other sustainability perspectives, art(s) education could benefit from considering pedagogical sustainability as a value basis. If one broadly understands sustainability as the wise use of resources, then pedagogical sustainability would be concerned with the tactful use of educational resources. Here, resources are not just restricted to money. Sustainable pedagogies would involve designing educational environments, contexts, and situations with an awareness of other sustainability dimensions. For instance, sustainable pedagogy could guide teachers to use instructional technology in environmentally conscious ways and balance its use with recognition of other sustainability perspectives without compromising the educational goals. Moreover, sustainable pedagogy could prevent attention waste and reduce fragmentation in learning situations while maintaining alignment with the broader processes of human growth and *Bildung*.

One possible way to evaluate the sustainability of learning situations is to use aesthetic criteria—an approach that should naturally align with art(s) educators' sensibilities. The aesthetic sustainability framework helps us examine how learning experiences can unfold as integrated with aesthetic value. In this context, Dewey's work on aesthetics provides an adept philosophical point of departure (see also Väkevä 2023a).

Adherents of *educational aesthetics* have especially found Dewey's ideas of aesthetic value worth analyzing in terms of how aesthetic qualities are ingrained in teaching-learning situations (Smith 2008). One of the most influential commentators in this field, Elliot Eisner, argued that creating educational experiences should be understood more as an art than as a science, which makes pedagogies subject to aesthetic evaluation (Eisner 1967, 1976, 2002, 2005, 2017). At the same time, educational aesthetics extends beyond teaching artistic values: since education aims to develop creative thinking in all fields, the aesthetic perspective remains relevant across all teaching subjects. Moreover, the aesthetic value of the educational process itself should be under scrutiny, and, according to Eisner, this requires a refined sense of *connoisseurship*, which can be interpreted as an ability to appreciate the full meaning of what one experiences (Eisner 1976).

Following Dewey (1996d), Eisner (2017) argues that aesthetic and artistic approaches help students recognize how elements of a whole relate to each other, not just in the arts but in any field of learning where elements must be meaningfully combined to make sense. An aesthetic approach can thus illuminate holistic aspects of phenomena that might not be accessible through language use alone. This is why Eisner suggests complementing education with artistic approaches: such approaches guide educators to adopt views that cultivate sensitivity to the aesthetic or qualitative aspects of life. For Eisner, this shift would not only improve educational quality but also help to develop the mindsets required to judge value in an increasingly complex world. From today's standpoint, they might also make sense as ecological approaches to human-environment entanglements.

In the Deweyan/Eisnerian outlook, art(s) education matters not only because it helps us to develop an understanding of the arts and aesthetic phenomena but also because it helps us to master the broader art of navigating complex circumstances—the art of living, as Dewey might say (Dewey 1996d, 339; see also Stroud 2011; Väkevä 2007). This holistic aesthetic perspective aligns well with sustainability education, as it guides us to seek ways to "exist 'well'" (Østern and Knudsen 2020, 5; see also Biesta 2018). An aesthetic educational perspective thus helps us envision art(s) education as a mediator in the lifelong journey of finding balanced ways of living, which can be identified with *Bildung*. Such balanced ways of living cannot emerge from instruction alone, nor can they be judged against any educational standards. On the contrary, as aesthetic education, art(s) education should avoid standardized measures of assessment used to measure system level 'performativity,' viz., performativity judged as a macro-level ability of an information management system to turn signs into capital, against which Jean-François Lyotard (1984) warned (see also Harari 2024). More specifically, Eisner (2017) contends that educational standards fail to properly evaluate meaningful growth in the art(s) since the latter deal primarily with qualities. Instead, we need to use flexible *criteria* that better capture the nuances of aesthetic experience across both arts and other fields. Understanding such criteria lies at the heart of educational connoisseurship. This approach naturally leads to embracing evaluation methods that can help us grasp the emergent qualities of artistic/educational processes (Väkevä 2019).

Significantly, from both Dewey's and Eisner's viewpoints, art's primary function is to express meanings rather than merely declare, state facts, or narrate, and such expressive meanings extend far beyond words. Here, we find a point of connection to what has been discussed above: While the voicings in art may disclose things, they should be understood primarily as performative acts that evoke meanings by making things happen. In human life, meanings are performed in many forms, only some of which can be captured by discursive symbol systems and algorithmic information processing. Others need to be directly experienced as qualitative phenomena. Educational aesthetics helps art(s) educators and their students focus on how things gain qualitative meaning within complex networks of relationships that may include a variety of actors, including GenAI. Yet, as far as we know, only sentient organisms experience such qualitative meanings and can share their aesthetic import in art. At the present state of technological development, it would probably be an idle effort to seek even traces of such sentience in AI despite its constantly growing creative capabilities.

Toward a Comprehensive Approach to the Pedagogical Sustainability of GenAI in Art(s) Education

The discussion above has revealed a potentially uncrossable boundary for AI: the qualitative realm of aesthetic meaning, which, in a Deweyan frame of reference, can be experienced only by sentient organisms. While all species probably share an aesthetic propensity, it only evolves into aesthetic-artistic taste in complex life forms, such as human culture. Art(s) education requires an awareness of this qualitative dimension of experience as well as a will to seek ways to support the students' innate abilities to find its significance in their lives.

In contrast, as AI models are based on algorithmic processes, they are functionally confined to the logic of optimizing their performance against predefined goals. This also applies to self-regulating systems such as GenAI models, the relative autonomy of which is achieved through additional algorithmic layers designed to adjust the models' operations to the user prompts or cues. As Sofian Audry (2021, 17) argues, this algorithmic logic fundamentally differs from art's operational principle since art, as art, has no objective evaluation function. Put differently, we cannot judge the value of art merely by its performative efficiency in causing other valuable things because its primary worth stems from enabling aesthetic experience in an expressive form, and aesthetic experience is qualitative and, thus, unique. Aesthetic judgments in art arise from how it unfolds within human experience, not from the artworks' instrumental purposefulness, even if art, of course, can also be used to reach external ends. The artistic process itself, when experienced aesthetically, reveals the value of the work undertaken, and following Dewey's thinking, this undertaking carries the artwork's aesthetic value forward through the varied experiences of its beholders. This explains why Dewey (1996d) discusses art *as* an experience rather than as merely something that causes or mediates it. When experienced aesthetically, art makes no claim to be something else but itself, namely, an aesthetic phenomenon.

While aesthetic quality has been emphasized above as primary determinant of artistic value, one should be cautious about interpreting the adjective 'aesthetic' too narrowly, as if it would only apply to the arts. Arguably, high modern conceptions of aesthetic value, being based on the tradition of the fine arts, cannot capture art's significance in late modern culture, as the latter, above all, values performativity as a sign of creativity and expects the domains of cultural production to be counted as significant on the neoliberal markets of attention (Reckwitz 2017, 2020a, 2020b, 2021). In a combined pragmatist and posthumanist interpretation, in such conditions, aesthetic taste goes beyond the mere judgment of beauty, harmony, or sublimity to reveal how quality permeates experience as things come to matter through performative acts. It is a matter of pedagogical judgment whether such emergent acts sustain aesthetic growth as the expanding capability to find qualitative value in life or if they merely support the attention economy.

Combining Deweyan and Baradian terminologies, one could argue that aesthetic quality always emerges in inquiry, which is based on an ability to detect how meanings emerge from mattering. At its best, art transforms mattering by revealing its expressive potential, which can be experienced as a quality that permeates the semiotic process unfolding in inquiry. All inquiries seek consummatory phases where problematic situations temporarily resolve themselves, leading to balanced states. Such balanced states are experienced as qualitative wholes. Rather than pointing to external goals, then, the aesthetic quality that emerges in inquiry is self-referential, pointing only to itself. As such, it offers a momentary resting place from further concerns and, ideally, also expands our horizons of meaning transactionally, as things will be momentarily put in a unified perspective (Alexander 1987). In such conditions, artistic voicing becomes transformative, as it educates the sense of the sensible.

To return to our main topic, the key question regarding the value of GenAI in art(s) education may not be whether it can lead us to have aesthetic experiences by generating new art. Instead, it might relate to how it participates in intra-actions that reveal the aesthetic potential invested in the lifeworld. Aesthetic meaning emerges in the dynamic interplay of agentive materiality that, through inquiry, gets to be organized and reorganized in ways that can be judged to be both educative and aesthetic. The main objective of aesthetically sustainable art(s) education using GenAI would be to help students recognize how meaning-making manifests as an experienced value when making and enjoying art, using aesthetic criteria rather than algorithmic standards to evaluate how such processes of making and enjoying lead to valuable outcomes. While comprehensive, this rationale hopefully helps to put GenAI in perspective, allowing us to avoid too hasty interpretations of its educative worth.

From the perspective of pedagogical sustainability, *tact* is essential in determining GenAI's role in education. This concept, borrowed from Max van Manen (1991, 2015), suggests that education contains a phronetic element of situational wisdom that helps educators attune to students' needs, adapting their pedagogical strategies in real-time prudently, even when they do not fully grasp the implications of their actions at the moment. Such tact is indispensable for cultivating pedagogical praxis and thus also contributes to pedagogically sustainable art(s) education. The perspective of educational aesthetics enriches tactful AI pedagogy by adding to it an evaluative dimension, reminding us to judge technology's pedagogical expediency by how it supports our pursuit of aesthetic meaning. In this context, pedagogical sustainability indicates thoughtfully using technological resources like GenAI to enhance students' sensitivity to aesthetic values that emerge through artistic inquiries.

References

Alexander, Thomas M. 1987. *John Dewey's Theory of Art, Experience, and Nature: The Horizons of Feeling*. Albany, NY: State University of New York Press.

Allen, Aaron S. 2019. Aesthetics and Sustainability. In *Encyclopedia of Sustainability in Higher Education*, ed. Walter Leal Filho, 25–33. Cham: Springer. https://doi.org/10.1007/978-3-030-11352-0_403.

Audry, Sofian. 2021. *Art in the Age of Learning Machines*. Cambridge, MA: The MIT Press.

Bentz, Julia, Leticia Do Carmo, Nicole Schafenacker, Jörn Schirok, and Sara D. Corso. 2022. Creative, Embodied Practices, and the Potentialities for Sustainability Transformations. *Sustainability Science* 17 (2): 687–699. https://doi.org/10.1007/s11625-021-01000-2.

Biesta, Gert. 2018. *Letting Art Teach. Art Education 'After' Joseph Beuys.* Arnhem: ArtEZ Press.

Bleher, Hannah, and Matthias Braun. 2023. Reflections on Putting AI Ethics into Practice: How Three AI Ethics Approaches Conceptualize Theory and Practice. *Science and Engineering Ethics* 29 (3): 21. https://doi.org/10.1007/s11948-023-00443-3.

Boddington, Paula. 2023. *AI Ethics: A Textbook.* Singapore: Springer. https://doi.org/10.1007/978-981-19-9382-4.

Boyer, Robert H. W., Nicole D. Peterson, Poonam Arora, and Kevin Caldwell. 2016. Five Approaches to Social Sustainability and an Integrated Way Forward. *Sustainability* 8 (9): 878. https://doi.org/10.3390/su8090878.

Callicott, J. Baird. 2018. Ecological Sustainability. In *A Sustainable Philosophy—The Work of Bryan Norton*, ed. Sahotra Sarkar and Ben A. Minteer, 27–47. Cham: Springer. https://doi.org/10.1007/978-3-319-92597-4_3.

Chen, Lin, Zhonghao Chen, Yubing Zhang, Yunfei Liu, Ahmed I. Osman, Mohamed Farghali, Jianmin Hua, Ahmed Al-Fatesh, Ikko Ihara, David W. Rooney, and Pow-Seng Yap. 2023. Artificial Intelligence-Based Solutions for Climate Change: A Review. *Environmental Chemistry Letters* 21 (5): 2525–2557. https://doi.org/10.1007/s10311-023-01617-y.

Clarke, Angela, and Shane Hulbert. 2016. Envisioning the Future: Working Toward Sustainability in Fine Art Education. *International Journal of Art & Design Education* 35 (1): 36–50. https://doi.org/10.1111/jade.12047.

Dellosa, Jeffrey T., and Eleonor C. Palconit. 2021. Artificial Intelligence (AI) in Renewable Energy Systems: A Condensed Review of Its Applications and Techniques. In *2021 IEEE International Conference on Environment and Electrical Engineering and 2021 IEEE Industrial and Commercial Power Systems Europe (EEEIC / I&CPS Europe)*, 1–6. https://doi.org/10.1109/EEEIC/ICPSEurope51590.2021.9584587.

Dewey, John. 1996d. *The Collected Works of John Dewey, 1882–1953 (2nd release). Electronic edition. The Later Works of John Dewey, 1925–1953.* Volume 10: 1934, Art as Experience. Carbondale and Edwardsville, IL/Charlottesville, VA: Southern Illinois University Press/InteLex.

Duany, Andres, Elizabeth Plater-Zyberk, and Jeff Speck. 2001. *Suburban Nation: The Rise of Sprawl and the Decline of the American Dream.* New York, NY: Macmillan.

Eisner, Elliot W. 1967. Educational Objectives: Help or Hindrance? *American Journal of Education* 91 (4): 549–560.

Eisner, Elliot W. 1976. Educational Connoisseurship and Criticism: Their Form and Functions in Educational Evaluation. *Journal of Aesthetic Education* 10 (3/4): 135–150. https://doi.org/10.2307/3332067.

Eisner, Elliot W. 2002. *The Arts and the Creation of Mind*. New Haven, CT: Yale University Press.

Eisner, Elliot W. 2005. *Reimagining Schools: The Selected Works of Elliot W. Eisner*. New York, NY: Routledge.

Eisner, Elliot W. 2017. *The Enlightened Eye: Qualitative Inquiry and the Enhancement of Educational Practice*. New York, NY: Teachers College Press.

Firt, Erez. 2024. What Makes Full Artificial Agents Morally Different. *AI & Society*. https://doi.org/10.1007/s00146-024-01867-6.

Foster, Raisa, Jussi Mäkelä, and Rebecca Martusewicz, eds. 2019. *Art, Ecojustice, and Education: Intersecting Theories and Practices*. London: Routledge.

Harari, Yuval Noah. 2024. *Nexus: A Brief History of Information Networks from the Stone Age to AI*. New York, NY: Random House.

Heinrichs, Harald, and Frank Biermann. 2016. Sustainability: Politics and Governance. In *Sustainability Science*, ed. Harald Heinrichs, Pim Martens, Gerd Michelsen, and Arnim Wiek, 129–137. Dodrecht: Springer. https://doi.org/10.1007/978-94-017-7242-6_11.

Heras, Maria. 2022. Art and Connectedness Within Sustainability: Educating Through Aesthetic Pedagogies. In *Competences in Education for Sustainable Development*, ed. Paul Vare, Nadia Lausselet, and Marco Rieckmann, 145–157. Cham: Springer. https://doi.org/10.1007/978-3-030-91055-6_18.

Illeris, Helene. 2012. Interrogations: Art, Art Education and Environmental Sustainability. *International Journal of Education Through Art* 8 (3): 221–237. https://doi.org/10.1386/eta.8.3.221_1.

Inwood, Hilary J., and Ryan W. Taylor. 2012. Creative Approaches to Environmental Learning: Two Perspectives on Teaching Environmental Art Education. *International Electronic Journal of Environmental Education* 2 (1): 65–75. https://files.eric.ed.gov/fulltext/EJ1057521.pdf.

Jain, Harshita, Renu Dhupper, Anamika Shrivastava, Deepak Kumar, and Maya Kumari. 2023. AI-Enabled Strategies for Climate Change Adaptation: Protecting Communities, Infrastructure, and Businesses from the Impacts of Climate Change. *Computational Urban Science* 3:25. https://doi.org/10.1007/s43762-023-00100-2.

Jeronen, Eila. 2020. Economic Sustainability. In *Encyclopedia of Sustainable Management*, ed. Samuel Idowu, Rene Schmidpeter, Nicholas Capaldi, Liangrong Zu, Mara Del Baldo, and Rute Abreu, 1–6. Cham: Springer. https://doi.org/10.1007/978-3-030-02006-4_197-1.

Lara, Francisco, and Jarn Deckers, eds. 2023. *Ethics of Artificial Intelligence*. Cham: Springer. https://doi.org/10.1007/978-3-031-48135-2.

Li, Pengfei, Jianyi Yang, Mohammad A. Islam, and Shaolei Ren. 2023. Making AI Less "Thirsty": Uncovering and Addressing the Secret Water Footprint of AI Models. https://doi.org/10.48550/ARXIV.2304.03271.

Luccioni, Alexandra S., Yacine Jernite, and Emma Strubell. 2023. Power Hungry Processing: Watts Driving the Cost of AI Deployment? https://doi.org/10.48550/ARXIV.2311.16863.

Lyotard, Jean-François. 1984. *The Postmodern Condition: A Report on Knowledge*. Minneapolis, MN: University of Minnesota Press.

Mantoan, Diego. 2021. Sustainability Way Beyond Academia Public Art as a Driver for Behavioural Change and the Participatory Quest of Gayle Chong Kwan: Public Art as a Driver for Behavioural Change and the Participatory Quest of Gayle Chong Kwan. In *Waste Matters Chronicles from a Food Archipelago in Venice*, I libri di Ca' Foscari, 15–29. Venezia: Fondazione Università Ca' Foscari. https://doi.org/10.30687/978-88-6969-576-6/001.

Mekonnen, Habtamu, Zemenu Bires, and Kessegn Berhanu. 2022. Practices and Challenges of Cultural Heritage Conservation in Historical and Religious Heritage Sites: Evidence from North Shoa Zone, Amhara Region, Ethiopia. *Heritage Science* 10 (1): 172. https://doi.org/10.1186/s40494-022-00802-6.

Nordgren, Anders. 2023. Artificial Intelligence and Climate Change: Ethical Issues. *Journal of Information, Communication and Ethics in Society* 21 (1): 1–15. https://doi.org/10.1108/JICES-11-2021-0106.

Open letter to President Biden from tech workers in Kenya. 2024, 22 May. https://www.foxglove.org.uk/open-letter-to-president-biden-from-tech-workers-in-kenya.

Østern, Anna-Lena, and Kristian N. Knudsen, eds. 2020. *Performative Approaches in Arts Education: Artful Teaching, Learning, and Research*. London: Routledge.

Pavlou, Victoria. 2024. *Critical ARts Education for Sustainable Societies: A Handbook for Arts Educators*. Cyprus: Frederick University.

Purvis, Ben, Yong Mao, and Darren Robinson. 2019. Three Pillars of Sustainability: In Search of Conceptual Origins. *Sustainability Science* 14 (3): 681–695. https://doi.org/10.1007/s11625-018-0627-5.

Raman, Raghu, Debidutta Pattnaik, Hiran H. Lathabai, Chandan Kumar, Kannan Govindan, and Prema Nedungadi. 2024. Green and Sustainable AI Research: An Integrated Thematic and Topic Modeling Analysis. *Journal of Big Data* 11:55. https://doi.org/10.1186/s40537-024-00920-x.

Reckwitz, Andreas. 2017. *The Invention of Creativity: Modern Society and the Culture of the New*. Cambridge: Polity.

Reckwitz, Andreas. 2020a. *The Society of Singularities*. Boston: De Gruyter.

Reckwitz, Andreas. 2020b. The Society of Singularities. In *Futures of the Study of Culture: Interdisciplinary Perspectives, Global Challenges*, ed. Doris Bachmann-Medick, Jens Kugele, and Ansgar Nünning, 141–154. Berlin: De Gruyter.

Reckwitz, Andreas. 2021. *The End of Illusions: Politics, Economy, and Culture in Late Modernity.* Cambridge: Polity.
Salonen, Arto O., and Jyrki Konkka. 2015. An Ecosocial Approach to Well-Being: A Solution to the Wicked Problems in the Era of Anthropocene. *Foro de Educación* 13 (19): 19–34. https://www.redalyc.org/pdf/4475/447544537003.pdf.
Sharma, Shalini. 2023. Cultivating Pedagogical Sustainability in Early Education. *International Journal of Management Education for Sustainable Development* 6 (6): 13–23. https://ijsdcs.com/index.php/IJMESD/article/view/320.
Shu, Lee-Lean. 2024. The Untold Story of AI's Huge Carbon Footprint. *Forbes*, 26 April. https://www.forbes.com/councils/forbestechcouncil/2024/04/26/the-untold-story-of-ais-huge-carbon-footprint/.
Smith, Ralph A. 2008. Educational Aesthetics and Policy. *Arts Education Policy Review* 109 (6): 3–12. https://doi.org/10.3200/AEPR.109.6.3-12.
Soini, Katriina, and Inger Birkeland. 2014. Exploring the Scientific Discourse on Cultural Sustainability. *Geoforum* 51:213–223. https://doi.org/10.1016/j.geoforum.2013.12.001.
Souza-Rodrigues, Eduardo. 2019. Deforestation in the Amazon: A Unified Framework for Estimation and Policy Analysis. *The Review of Economic Studies* 86 (6): 2713–2744. https://doi.org/10.1093/restud/rdy070.
Stahl, Bernd C., Doris Schroeder, and Rowena Rodrigues. 2023. *Ethics of Artificial Intelligence: Case Studies and Options for Addressing Ethical Challenges.* Cham: Springer. https://link.springer.com/book/10.1007/978-3-031-17040-9.
Stephenson, Janet. 2023. *Culture and Sustainability: Exploring Stability and Transformation with the Cultures Framework.* Cham: Springer. https://doi.org/10.1007/978-3-031-25515-1.
Stroud, Scott R. 2011. *John Dewey and the Artful Life: Pragmatism, Aesthetics, and Morality.* University Park, PN: Pennsylvania State University Press.
Trott, Carlie D., Trevor L. Even, and Susan M. Frame. 2020. Merging the Arts and Sciences for Collaborative Sustainability Action: A Methodological Framework. *Sustainability Science* 15 (4): 1067–1085. https://doi.org/10.1007/s11625-020-00798-7.
Vacchi, Marco, Cristina Siligardi, Fabio Demaria, Erika I. Cedillo-González, Rocio González-Sánchez, and Davide Settembre-Blundo. 2021. Technological Sustainability or Sustainable Technology? A Multidimensional Vision of Sustainability in Manufacturing. *Sustainability* 13 (17): 9942. https://doi.org/10.3390/su13179942.
Väkevä, Lauri. 2007. Art Education, The Art of Education and the Art of Life: Considering the Implications of Dewey's Later Philosophy to Art and Music Education. *Action, Criticism & Theory for Music Education* 6 (1): 1–15. https://act.maydaygroup.org/articles/Vakeva6_1.pdf.
Väkevä, Lauri. 2019. Evaluation for Equality: Applying a Classical Pragmatist Perspective in Qualitative Assessment in Finnish General Music Education. In

The Oxford Handbook of Philosophical and Qualitative Assessment in Music Education, ed. David J. Elliott, Marissa Silverman, and Gary E. McPherson, 100–121. New York, NY: Oxford University Press. https://doi.org/10.1093/oxfordhb/9780190265182.013.7.

Väkevä, Lauri. 2023a. *Considering Deweyan Cultural Naturalism as a Philosophy of Art(s) Education: Restoring Continuity*. Cham: Springer. https://doi.org/10.1007/978-3-031-38817-0.

Väkevä, Lauri. 2023b. Kestävyysajattelu musiikkikasvattajan ammatillisen refektiivisyyden haastajana [Challenging the Professional Reflectivity of Music Educator with Sustainability Thinking]. In *Musiikkikasvatus muutoksessa* [*Music Education in Transformation*], ed. Marja-Leena Juntunen, and Heidi Partti, 479–500. Helsinki: DocMus Research Publications 20, Sibelius Academy of the University of the Arts Helsinki. https://taju.uniarts.fi/bitstream/handle/10024/7961/e-pdf_Musiikkikasvatus%20muutoksessa_Sibelius-Akatemia.pdf?sequence=1&isAllowed=y.

Väkevä, Lauri, and Heidi Partti. 2025 (in print). Towards AI Didactics: Call for Teachers to Train Large Language Models for Research Writing in Higher Arts Education. In *Education and Artificial Intelligence Handbook*, ed. Guy Tchibozo. Cham: Springer.

Van Manen, Max. 1991. *The Tact of Teaching: The Meaning of Pedagogical Thoughtfulness*. Albany, NY: State University of New York Press.

Van Manen, Max. 2015. *Pedagogical tact: Knowing What to Do When You Don't Know What to Do*. Milton Park: Routledge.

Van Wynsberghe, Aimee. 2021. Sustainable AI: AI for Sustainability and the Sustainability of AI. *AI and Ethics* 1 (3): 213–218. https://doi.org/10.1007/s43681-021-00043-6.

Verdecchia, Roberto, June Sallou, and Luis Cruz. 2023. A Systematic Review of Green AI. https://doi.org/10.48550/ARXIV.2301.11047.

Whittlestone, Jess, and Samuel Clarke. 2022. AI Challenges for Society and Ethics. In *The Oxford Handbook of AI Governance*, ed. Justin B. Bullock, Yu-Che Chen, Johannes Himmelreich, Valerie M. Hudson, Anton Korinek, Matthew M. Young, and Baobao Zhang, 45–64. New York, NY: Oxford University Press. https://doi.org/10.1093/oxfordhb/9780197579329.013.3.

Wu, Carole-Jean, Ramya Raghavendra, Udit Gupta, Bilge Acun, Newsha Ardalani, Kiwan Maeng, Gloria Chang, Fiona A. Behram, James Huang, Charles Bai, Michael Gschwind, Anurag Gupta, Myle Ott, Anastasia Melnikov, Salvatire Candido, David Brooks, Geeta Chauhan, Benjamin Lee, Hsien-Hsin Lee, Akyildiz Bugra, Maximilian Balandat, Joe Spisak, Ravi Jain, Mike Rabbat, and Kim Hazelwood. 2021. Sustainable AI: Environmental Implications, Challenges and Opportunities. https://doi.org/10.48550/ARXIV.2111.00364.

CHAPTER 5

The Multimodal Voicings of GenAI

Abstract This chapter further discusses GenAI as a voicing agent, focusing on the capabilities of Multimodal Large Language Models (MLLMs) in art(s) education. While these models obviously implicate sustainability challenges, they can also forge pathways for transdisciplinary artistic exploration. The increasing capability of AI to operate autonomously needs to be studied by art(s) educators carefully to support the building of the students' critical AI literacy.

Keywords Artificial intelligence • Voicing • Multimodality • Art education • Transdisciplinarity • Literacy

The Pros and Cons of Multimodality: From Representation to Presentation

With their "ability to receive, reason, and output multimodal information" (Yin et al. 2024), cutting-edge MLLMs can process and transform diverse types of content, including images, audio, music, and video. Specialized AI tools have developed similar capabilities, as exemplified by platforms like Runway and Krea, which allow users to convert static images into video and vice versa using existing images or videos as seeds. Some multimodal models can even create sound and music from images and vice

L. Väkevä, *Voicing Responsible AI Pedagogy for Music and Visual Arts Education*, https://doi.org/10.1007/978-3-031-86410-0_5

versa, with or without text prompts (Hisariya et al. 2024; Rinaldi et al. 2024). This expansion beyond simple unimodal conversions creates a rich space of creative opportunities where different modes of expression feed each other, fostering hybrid art forms.

However, as discussed above, the widespread use of GenAI models also raises significant sustainability concerns that require recognition in tactful art(s) education. The operation of MLLMs and their supporting hardware demands substantial energy resources. In addition, these models are susceptible to manipulation and frequently reflect biases present in their training data, potentially generating content that causes representational harm if interpreted as referring to reality. The current mediasphere is filled with GenAI-produced deepfakes, and research shows that such artificial content influences behavior even when its inauthenticity is recognized (see, e.g., Lundberg and Mozelius 2024). This phenomenon has a precedent in the effects of AI-filtered disinformation spread through social media, which has triggered political polarization and even caused ethnic conflicts (Amnesty 2022). Some commentators predict such harmful effects will intensify as AI becomes a primary creator of media content, both generating and moderating material on its own (Harari 2024). Some artists have also argued that GenAI-produced content will eventually blur the line between human and AI-based art, leading to a situation that distances artistic practice and audience sensibilities from the historical context of artmaking.[1]

However, as discussed above, focusing solely on GenAI art's epistemic inaccuracy may miss a crucial point. When studied in creative contexts, these models may primarily serve a performative rather than an epistemic function. Instead of expecting GenAI to represent external reality or continue the mimetic traditions of art history, we can maybe understand it as a creative force that presents new information and expressive modes—information and expressive modes that, of course, become meaningful only when interpreted within specific cultural contexts by agents capable

[1] For instance, Finnish designer and comics artist Ville Tietäväinen claimed in December 2024 that we are "creating an AIcene, an epoch, that does not leave the truth to upcoming humanity and changes the history so far to its own mockery" (Tietäväinen 2024, translation by the author). In a broader context, Everton Gomede (2024) has claimed that "AIcene" provides impacts that are "both promising and dangerous, raising questions about the future of human society and the potential risks of relying heavily on AI technologies." Whether AI really changes the conditions of the Anthropocene remains to be seen.

of such interpretation. From this perspective, the output of GenAI does not even aim to narrate reality but rather offers new ways to experience it.

As has been argued above, this interpretation becomes particularly interesting in cases in which GenAI uses cloned human voices. As AI users increasingly engage with advanced voice models, they perhaps enter liminal spaces where they interact with AI actants as if the latter had genuine voices, diminishing the sense of uncanniness that previously accompanied encounters with too-human-like technologies. Indeed, for many, conversational AI has already become an advisor, therapist, and even romantic partner (Abrams 2023; Li and Zhang 2024). Especially representatives of the post-millennial generation seem to be not too concerned whether they are communicating with AI or a human being, as long as the interaction serves their needs, despite the apparent fact that many young people are acutely conscious of the associated sustainability risks (Chan and Lee 2023; see also Leonard 2020). The rising popularity of such conversational AI models as Character.ai has prompted GenAI developers to enhance the human-like communication capabilities of these technologies, transforming human-AI interaction into an entanglement between ostensibly equal agents. A similar shift may be occurring in the reception of art, leading us to accept that AI-produced artworks are not merely fakes but, instead, expressions of alternative voices (see also Danesi 2024).

Transdisciplinary Voicings of AI in Art(s) Education

Performing as a multimodal content transformer, GenAI can help artists transcend traditional disciplinary boundaries, moving between different techniques and forms of expression. By leveraging GenAI's ability to transform one modality into another, artists can also explore new creative domains in ways that were previously difficult or even impossible to fathom (Pareschi 2024a, 2024b). This not only expands the artists' toolkits but also enables them to forge pathways for transdisciplinary artistic exploration.

'Transdisciplinary' here indicates that the artistic inquiries committed not only take place on several creative domains at the same time but also create new ones, surpassing traditional disciplinary boundaries. To use Deweyan vocabulary, the cross-pollination of ideas, approaches, and methods across artistic domains leads to inquiries that would not be possible within single-discipline frameworks, as the problems triggering such inquiries are more complex. This leads to transactions that transform the conditions of further action. Such transactions can take place both between artistic domains and between artistic and other domains, generating novel ideas, contexts, and even new epistemic regimes. For instance, examples of such transdisciplinary art forms might include AI installations and real-time animations in which viewers play an active role (Cheng et al. 2023; Lin et al. 2023). Recent examples of art-science hybrids include such approaches as the AmalGAN project of Alexander Reben (2019), which transforms the body signals into paintings, and the brain-scanning art of the Obvious trio (Chen 2024), as well as the numerous scientific research projects in which artists play a significant part (Gould 2023).

What implications does all this transdisciplinary experimentation have for art(s) education? Using GenAI to work across artistic practices and between arts and other inquiries provides new opportunities to explore connections between teaching subjects and inspires cross-disciplinary or integrative curricula. This suggests that GenAI might support *phenomenon-based learning*, which begins not from discipline-specific problems but applies diverse inquiries to study common challenges (see Schaffar and Wolff 2024). Sustainability issues provide one widely recognized problem area for such transdisciplinary approaches.

Another viable field for transdisciplinary art(s) education is media literacies. In today's postdigital mediasphere, traditional creative boundaries are dissolving through technological mediation, creating a need to develop multimodal literacy skills—skills that enable students to navigate and interpret the complex semiotic landscapes of contemporary media (Mills and Unsworth 2017). GenAI's role as a multimodal creative agent may transform our understanding of media literacy, moving beyond conventional frameworks of decoding and interpretation. The performative capabilities of multimodal GenAI may even enact entirely new approaches to 'reading' that recognize the pragmatist nature of all semiotic agencies. Instead of seeing meaning as purely representational, we might pay attention to how it emerges through patterns of intra-actions where machines play an increasingly more significant role, reshaping what Dewey might call 'experiential continuity' and what Rancière termed the 'distribution of the sensible.' In such aesthetic ecologies, the locus of interpretation of meaning is not always self-evident; meaning becomes a field event, interpretable only through participation of the networked actors that make it possible.

As a performative agent, GenAI also potentially transforms the relationship between artists and technology, providing instances of what

Remo Pareschi calls "centaur art"—a hybrid form of art that transcends modern distinctions between media and message (Pareschi 2024a, 2024b). Pareschi (2024b) even anticipates that 'centauric' operations between humans and self-adaptive technologies will change the conditions of human being, heralding an evolutionary progression from *Homo sapiens*, with innate cognitive abilities, to *Homo faber*, which uses technology to transform the environment, to *Centaurus Faber*, which hybridizes human and artificial intelligence. Such transhumanist forecasts might not seem that utopian in the age of rapidly developing AI voicing.

Rather than merely providing tools to support artistic creativity, then, GenAI offers human-machine partnerships that transcend the Heideggerian notion of a tool as something that is at hand, offering itself ready to be used for humane purposes (Heidegger 2010, 67–71; see also Harman 2002; Kondor 2016; Leonard 2020). This shift potentially challenges traditional roles of technology in artistic practice and raises essential questions about who the author is. Allegedly, these changing role distributions within the art-based actor-networks are best understood by moving from modern, human-centered frameworks of creativity toward a late modern posthumanist perspective that allows for distributed creativities between human and non-human (or more-than-human) agents.

Indeed, as artists become accustomed to working with GenAI, their role may shift from creators to curators or editors, with AI tools increasingly handling the basic manipulation of expressive material, functioning like contemporary versions of artists' apprentices. This transformation prompts us to rethink artistic creativity as the lines blur between creator and creation and between human and machine contribution (Park 2023, 2024). For art(s) education, this means paying attention to how human and machine agencies form symbiotic relationships in actor-networks, shifting the ontological frames toward the centauric model (Pareschi 2024a, 2024b). While AI art began as a human enterprise, we may soon witness AI developing greater creative autonomy, offering its own interpretations of the art it creates, and eventually creating art for its own purposes. This suggests that developing technical literacy alone is insufficient for students to understand the role GenAI in (the) art(s); they need to be prepared for its emerging independent agency. Students also need a broad understanding of AI's origins, development, and the conditions of its use in different contexts. Transdisciplinary approaches that acknowledge AI's creative autonomy seem to offer the best foundation for anticipating how GenAI will shape artistic practices in the future.

References

Abrams, Zara. 2023. AI Is Changing Every Aspect of Psychology. Here's What to Watch for. *Monitor on Psychology* 54 (5): 46. https://www.apa.org/monitor/2023/07/psychology-embracing-ai.

Amnesty. 2022. The Social Atrocity: Meta and the Right to Remedy for the Rohingya. https://www.amnesty.org/en/documents/ASA16/5933/2022/en/.

Chan, Cecilia K. Y., and Katherine K. W. Lee. 2023. The AI Generation Gap: Are Gen Z Students More Interested in Adopting Generative AI Such as ChatGPT in Teaching and Learning Than Their Gen X and Millennial Generation Teachers? *Smart Learning Environments* 10 (1): 60. https://doi.org/10.1186/s40561-023-00269-3.

Chen, Min. 2024. French Collective Obvious Has Created an A.I. Art Generator That Can Read Your Mind. *Artnet*, 14 May. https://news.artnet.com/art-world/obvious-mind-to-image-ai-2486868.

Cheng, Mingyong, Xuexi Dang, and Zetao Yu. 2023. Fusion: Landscape and Beyond 2.0: An Interactive AI Generated Art Installation. *ACM SIGGRAPH Asia 2023 Art Gallery*, 1–2. https://doi.org/10.1145/3610537.3622954.

Danesi, Marcel. 2024. *AI-Generated Popular Culture: A Semiotic Perspective*. New York, NY: Palgrave Macmillan.

Gomede, Everton. 2024. AIcene: A New Epoch in Human History. *Medium*, 25 August. https://medium.com/the-modern-scientist/aicene-a-new-epoch-in-human-history-9793f443d2d9.

Gould, Julie. 2023. Art and Science: Close Cousins or Polar Opposites? *Nature*, 3 November. https://doi.org/10.1038/d41586-023-03389-5.

Harari, Yuval Noah. 2024. *Nexus: A Brief History of Information Networks from the Stone Age to AI*. New York, NY: Random House.

Harman, Graham. 2002. *Tool-Being: Heidegger and the Metaphysics of Objects*. Chicago, IL: Open Court.

Heidegger, Martin. 2010. *Being and Time*. Albany, NY: State University of New York Press.

Hisariya, Tanisha, Huan Zhang, and Jinhua Liang. 2024. Bridging Paintings and Music—Exploring Emotion based Music Generation Through Paintings. https://doi.org/10.48550/arXiv.2409.07827.

Kondor, Zsuzanna. 2016. New Media, Old Concerns: Heidegger Revisited. In *Philosophy of Emerging Media*, ed. Juliet Floyd and James E. Katz, 132–145. New York, NY: Oxford University Press. https://doi.org/10.1093/acprof:oso/9780190260743.003.0008.

Leonard, Nicholas. 2020. Entanglement Art Education: Factoring ARTificial Intelligence and Nonhumans into Future Art Curricula. *Art Education* 73 (4): 22–28. https://doi.org/10.1080/00043125.2020.1746163.

Li, Han, and Renwen Zhang. 2024. Finding Love in Algorithms: Deciphering the Emotional Contexts of Close Encounters with AI Chatbots. *Journal of Computer-Mediated Communication* 29 (5): zmae015. https://doi.org/10.1093/jcmc/zmae015.

Lin, Rem R., Yongen Ke, and Kang Zhang. 2023. Urban Symphony: An AI and Data-Driven Approach to Real-Time Animation for Public Digital Art. In *Proceedings of the 16th International Symposium on Visual Information Communication and Interaction*, ed. Roger Malina, Zhang Kang, Zheng Wei, and Günter Wallner, 1–7. https://doi.org/10.1145/3615522.3615553.

Lundberg, Ebba, and Peter Mozelius. 2024. The Potential Effects of Deepfakes on News Media and Entertainment. *AI & Society*. https://doi.org/10.1007/s00146-024-02072-1.

Mills, Kathy A., and Len Unsworth. 2017. Multimodal Literacy. In *Oxford Research Encyclopedia of Education*, ed. K.A. Mills and L. Unsworth. Oxford: Oxford University Press. https://doi.org/10.1093/acrefore/9780190264093.013.232.

Pareschi, Remo. 2024a. Beyond Human and Machine: An Architecture and Methodology Guideline for Centaurian Design. *Sci* 6 (4): 71. https://doi.org/10.3390/sci6040071.

Pareschi, Remo. 2024b. *Centaur Art: The Future of Art in the Age of Generative AI*. Cham: Springer. https://doi.org/10.1007/978-3-031-69063-1.

Park, Sungijn. 2024. The Work of Art in the Age of Generative AI: Aura, Liberation, and Democratization. *AI & Society*. https://doi.org/10.1007/s00146-024-01948-6.

Park, Ye S. 2023. Creative and Critical Entanglements with AI in Art Education. *Studies in Art Education* 64 (4): 406–425. https://doi.org/10.1080/00393541.2023.2255084.

Reben, Alexander. 2019. AmalGAN. https://areben.com/project/amalgan/.

Rinaldi, Ivan, Nicola Fanelli, Giovanna Castellano, and Gennaro Vessio. 2024. Art2Mus: Bridging Visual Arts and Music Through Cross-Modal Generation. 10.48550/arXiv.2410.04906.

Schaffar, Birgit, and Lili-Ann Wolff. 2024. Phenomenon-Based Learning in Finland: A Critical Overview of Its Historical and Philosophical Roots. *Cogent Education* 11 (1): 2309733. https://doi.org/10.1080/2331186X.2024.2309733.

Tietäväinen, Ville. 2024. Olemme luomassa epookkia, joka muuttaa historian irvikuvakseen [We Are Creating an Epoch That Changes History to Its Mockery]. *Helsingin Sanomat*, 17 December. https://www.hs.fi/mielipide/art-2000010905128.html.

Yin, Shukang, Chaoyu Fu, Shirui Zhao, Ke Li, Xing Sun, Tong Xu, and Enhong Chen. 2024. A Survey on Multimodal Large Language Models. *National Science Review* 11 (12): nwae403. https://doi.org/10.1093/nsr/nwae403.

CHAPTER 6

Troubling Art(s) Pedagogy with Gen AI

Abstract This chapter focuses on the use of GenAI in art(s) education in relation to traditional didactic approaches to teaching. A central theme emerges from this discussion: AI's potential to disrupt conventional teaching practices. The chapter suggests a new way to envision how adaptive technologies can engage in the didactic relationship between teaching, learning, and subject matter. However, it also argues that even if AI can learn, instruct, and maybe grow with us, it cannot educate; for that, a tactful human educator is needed.

Keywords Artificial intelligence • Art education • Didactics • Disruption • Teaching • Learning • Educational theory

The Impact of GenAI on Artistic Practices

The integration of technology into the arts potentially transforms how art is learned. New technological tools provide new avenues for gaining skills, knowledge, and understanding within creative domains. Each technological advancement arguably enhances artistic creativity and, thus, expands the boundaries of particular artistic practices. Yet, until recent years, technological tools have required human agency to direct the creative process.

As clarified above, GenAI represents a fundamental shift in this trajectory. Unlike previous AI technologies that served primarily as tools to

L. Väkevä, *Voicing Responsible AI Pedagogy for Music and Visual Arts Education*, https://doi.org/10.1007/978-3-031-86410-0_6

enhance human creativity, GenAI introduces a new semi-autonomous actor into the artistic workflow. Platforms like DALL-E, Stable Diffusion, and Flux for visual arts, as well as AIVA, Suno, and Udio for music, can generate original content with minimal direct human contribution. This challenges traditional notions of authorship, originality, and ownership of the creative process. The semi-autonomous capabilities of GenAI models also transform the conditions of disseminating and enjoying art as intelligent algorithms increasingly direct and filter the data flow. All this raises serious questions about whether art(s) education needs to adjust to the new circumstances.

As discussed above, GenAI also presents significant sustainability concerns regarding, for example, its ecological footprint, pre-training, and the cultural bias of the data on which it has been instructed. Such sustainability issues call for transdisciplinary inquiries about the long-term viability of integrating GenAI into creative workflows. They also underscore the need for devising more sustainable AI pedagogies for artists and art(s) educators. According to the stance developed in this book, such pedagogies should be informed by critical AI literacy—a set of understandings that help us confront various challenges related to the development, training, and use of these technologies (see, e.g., Mills et al. 2024; Mills and Unsworth 2017; Ng et al. 2021; Pinski and Benlian 2024). An essential part of such literacy is an understanding of how AI disrupts traditional artistic and educational practices.

Disrupting Educational Praxis with GenAI

How does GenAI disrupt art(s) education? In addition to its apparent transformative power to change how art is practiced, disseminated, and enjoyed, it arguably alters the didactic relationship between the student, teacher, and subject matter by bringing in a new active element (see also Dasari et al. 2024; Väkevä and Partti 2025). Thus, GenAI affects the triadic balance of the didactic set-up, troubling the traditional emphasis on the teacher's pedagogical impact on the relationship between the student and the subject matter. This is in line with the suggestion of some educational scholars to expand the didactic triangle to a didactic tetrahedron that adds a technological element to the pedagogical situation (see

Augustsson and Boström 2016; Dasari et al. 2024; Goodchild and Sriraman 2012; Rezat and Sträßer 2012; Ruthven 2012; Tall 1986).[1]

Where art students have traditionally engaged with the poietic aspects of their discipline—e.g., learning how to create music, edit video, or outline images—GenAI now enables them to bypass many of these steps, as it minimizes the human effort required to manipulate artistic materials directly. For example, in a music class, the student might use a GenAI tool like Suno to generate a series of multi-instrumental compositions from a seed or a prompt, bypassing the need to learn traditional compositional skills for organizing musical materials expressively. This shifts the center of gravity from hands-on musical learning to meta-level skills. Instead of technical mastery, students now need to develop a critical ability to evaluate GenAI output, filter and curate its most appealing elements, and edit these elements to achieve satisfying aesthetic outcomes. These meta-level skills more closely resemble the abilities of music producers than the traditional roles of composers or songwriters.

In a similar vein, visual art students can create images by merely describing their ideas to GenAI or guiding the tool with seed pictures, videos, or even audio or music. For example, using a platform like Krea, a student might craft a detailed imaginary landscape by inputting descriptive prompt phrases or curating seed images from a variety of sources for the system to blend. In such platforms, it is also possible to see the results of developing artistic prompting in real-time, using the combination of user-end guidance and seeds to observe how the AI model generates art. Such multipurpose tools also make it easy to develop video content and combine video scenes with narrative structures.[2]

[1] The adjective 'didactic' here simply refers to the art and discipline of teaching. The didactic triangle is a classical way to display the interactions taking place in teaching situations. Initially based on Johann Friedrich Herbart's *Erziehungslehre*, such educational theorists as Paul Heimann used it to outline the interpersonal encounter in the pedagogical situation (Wiesner et al. 2023). Later, there have been different attempts to extend the didactic triangle, of which the didactic tetrahedron is one.

[2] Such generative practices of image-making were already experimented with in the 2010s e.g., by Alexander Mordvintsev, who studied how GANs, or Generative Adversarial Networks, 'dream' images based on the ability of multi-level neural networks to gradually regenerate pre-trained image patterns, often resulting in surprising outcomes (see Alexander Mordvintsev 2024). Later, GANs were developed into Creative Adversarial Networks or CANs, that were able to generate artworks from other works of art by learning about styles yet often deviating from the learned styles to create new creative ideas (Elgammal et al. 2017; Miller 2019).

From the standpoint of pedagogical sustainability, a crucial aspect of AI-supported art(s) education is the educator's ability to train, supervise, and guide GenAI models to enhance the student's learning, growth, and *Bildung*. Arguably, such meta-level didactic competence is an essential part of art(s) educators' critical AI literacy, as well, meaning that art(s) educators must both educate students and instruct GenAI to support their learning process (Väkevä and Partti 2025). While AI guidance initially centered on crafting and managing text-based prompts (Bozkurt 2023), new multimodal opportunities available through MLLMs expand it to include the guiding of models with diverse inputs, such as visual and auditory cues. Directing GenAI also requires an understanding of how to refine prompts based on system responses—a process that can be intricate and detailed, as various AI artists have documented (see, e.g., Hutson and Cotroneo 2023; Ploin et al. 2024).[3]

Additionally, GenAI users can create local models trained with their own data. This enables the personalization of AI assistants for various purposes, such as analyzing color palettes, creating lyrics in particular musical genres, and even emulating the student's idiomatic artistic style. If the use of such local models will increase in the arts, art(s) educators should also be able to teach their students how to prompt them. Indeed, AI scholars predict that creative AI will increasingly rely on purpose-tailored assistants, which, when coordinated, can become parts of more complex AI agents capable of handling multiple functions simultaneously (Gao et al. 2023; Gates 2023).[4]

Since foundational GenAI models' pre-training data encompasses an extensive and diverse repertoire of artistic styles, techniques, and historical traditions from across cultures and periods, these models can serve as sources of creative inspiration and artistic exploration if tactfully implemented. Rather than focusing solely on traditional style guidance and technical instruction, teachers can now take on a more facilitative role, helping students navigate, mix, and meaningfully engage with artistic traditions in ways that resonate with their idiosyncratic creative voices and artistic aspirations. This shift in pedagogical approach aligns naturally with contemporary art practices, where personal expression and individual

[3] AI artists have also been discussed as 'prompt artists,' highlighting the role of prompting in the creative process (Chang et al. 2023).

[4] Creating such assistants and agents has become easy as GenAI systems now handle the basic coding, allowing users to focus on tasks rather than technical details.

creative vision often take precedence over demonstrating technical mastery of documented traditions (see, e.g., Audry 2021; Rancière 2012). The vast array of styles and techniques accessible through GenAI can thus serve as a springboard for students to discover new artistic approaches and develop artistic identities.

MLLMs further expand AI's impact on how students engage with hybrid art forms. For instance, students can experiment with transforming musical pieces into visual art by converting audio data to abstract images and vice versa. They can also turn static images into video using generative tools like Runway, Luma, or Sora. With modern editing platforms such as Krea and LXT Studio, students can also combine various visual and audio sources to create videos and narrative films. These multimodal platforms enable cross-disciplinary art projects, encouraging innovative approaches to hybrid artmaking and pushing students beyond traditional disciplinary boundaries.

While GenAI ostensibly democratizes access to creative tools, it may also reduce students' engagement with traditional discipline-based principles of art(s) education, such as working hands-on with tactile materials in the plastic arts. Yet, it can be argued that new media arts have already transformed the conditions of this involvement by introducing contexts where students depend on digital tools to operate with artistic subject matter. In the postdigital culture, direct involvement with material becomes increasingly distanced due to assisting technologies (Berry and Dieter 2015; Knox 2019; Tavin et al. 2021). In such conditions, art(s) educators need to find new ways to help students work with materials, actualizing the agentive potential of the data processing aesthetically. As suggested above, one way to do this would be to focus on the performativity of artistic-material entanglements of actor-networks that involve both human and AI agents.

For art(s) educators, GenAI's disruption of artistic practices thus raises significant questions: How should teachers adapt their methods to account for GenAI's active role as a creative partner in the praxis of education? How can they evaluate students' work aesthetically when the line between human and machine creativity becomes increasingly blurred? What makes an AI artwork the work of the student? Who is its author? Does it even matter?—Addressing such questions may require a critical rethinking of pedagogical models inherited from inherited disciplines to ensure that students learn not only to use GenAI in making, disseminating, and enjoying art but also to engage with AI critically, keeping an eye on its performative potential. As discussed above, a way ahead could be to discard the modern theoretical notion of the didactic teacher-student-content triangle and instead seek new didactic models inspired by pragmatist and posthumanist philosophies, where learning is seen as an active engagement with semiotic entanglements of a variety of actors. In a more extensive outlook, such ecological didactic models could maybe help us see learning, growth, and *Bildung* as field events where intra-actions between various kinds of agents constantly create new possibilities for meaning-making, culminating in new habits of action.

A Call for Pedagogical Agency in Support of *Bildung*

While creativity in the arts can no longer be narrowed only to human agency, and GenAI seems to be able to act in the role of an instructor in many situations previously requiring human input, it can be argued that human mediators are still needed in pedagogical contexts to support *Bildung*. This is because *Bildung* is a life-long process of identity formation and cultivation bolstered by pedagogical relationships between individuals operating in a shared lifeworld, involving roles that machine agents cannot entirely displace, at least not yet.

However, from the standpoint of posthumanist philosophy, this argumentation might be seen faulty, for, at least on the surface, it requires returning to the modern idea(l) of human agency being qualitatively unique among various life forms and also ontologically distinct from non-human agencies, including the agencies of machines. Thus, it also raises the question of whether the concept of *Bildung* still has relevance in a networked late modern information society, the culture of which is increasingly produced, disseminated, and consumed through technological mediation that seemingly transcends such binary positionalities.

This might also be reformulated as a question of what kind of agency is needed to support *Bildung* when dealing with GenAI. It was argued above that a teacher's technical proficiency is not sufficient for developing critical AI literacy in art(s) education. Instead, pedagogical sustainability ushers the teacher to pay attention to how the didactic interactions can be turned into semiotic transactions, creating new habits of action on the basis of diverse intra-actions that provide a material ground for artistic teaching-learning and growth processes. A constructive approach to

GenAI-integrated art(s) education would seem to require a pedagogical strategy that balances technical proficiency with critical engagement and ethical reflection, which, as discussed above, self-adapting technologies cannot yet accomplish by themselves. Such a pedagogy would:

- Encourage students to view GenAI as a collaborator rather than a replacement for human agency, fostering a mindset that accepts co-creativity between human and machine agencies.
- Combine human creativity with AI creativity, seeking ways to find meaning in a variety of entanglements made possible by combined human and AI agencies.
- Provide opportunities for critical reflection on the implications of GenAI in the arts, such as its impact on originality, authorship, cultural values, and accessibility.

Such an approach would thus cultivate the student's ability to think critically about the role of GenAI in artistic practices and, more broadly, the role of art (and the arts) in the networks that provide meaning in human life. It would also help to facilitate pedagogical sustainability, both in the sense that educational resources would be used sustainably and in the sense that the developing AI literacy would include elements of eco-social *Bildung*, which can be here interpreted as a process where the students construct a recognition of the interdependencies between various spheres of life as a basis for their own sustainable lives (Salonen and Brady 2015).

Indeed, ignoring the need to build eco-social awareness when working with GenAI would risk several adversarial outcomes. For instance, students may become overly reliant on AI tools, treating them as epistemic (or, indeed, pedagogical) authorities rather than performative collaborators. They may also be content to generate content with these tools rather than use them to compose works in which they can recognize their handprint. Art(s) educators, meanwhile, may struggle to integrate GenAI effectively into their pedagogical praxes, underutilizing its educative potential or failing to address its ethical and creative challenges. All this points to superficial educational uses of AI, which neglects its semiotic potential in human-machine entanglements. To navigate these risks, art(s) pedagogics must encourage students to question and reflect on their use of GenAI in real-life situations where art is created, mediated, and enjoyed. Such an approach requires a human contribution to the growth processes. In such entanglements, human educators become more than instructors or teachers; they serve as stewards and caretakers of human growth, acting in roles that cannot be passed on to algorithmic systems. Even in a posthumanist world, it seems, human agency is needed if one wants to support *Bildung*.

Can AI Educate?

As suggested above, educating for *Bildung* requires a capacity for ethical deliberation—an ability that appears beyond AI's reach both now and in the foreseeable future. While GenAI models and other self-adaptive technologies can communicate with us and learn and instruct us in ways that would have seemed utopian some years ago, their potential to support *Bildung* remains questionable. Though AI systems, being built on the deep learning of multi-leveled neural networks, can rapidly expand their neural connections, thus gaining agency in the semiotic spaces they share with humans, it remains uncertain whether they will ever be capable of judging their operations based on ethical values. They seem to be ethical agents only via their capability to emulate human behavior.

But can AI systems not support human growth? For Dewey (1996a), the ability to grow means engaging with new challenges and opportunities, which, in his books, is the essence of being alive. Growth, for Dewey, is also a social ideal: it requires value-based communication and coordination of action within a society, thriving best in democratic ways of life that ensure maximal free exchange of ideas among peers without risking its political premises. Growing in this sense requires cultivating critical thinking habits, ethical deliberation, and an imaginative openness to envision new future experiences. Importantly, Dewey also saw growth as open-ended, suggesting that it denotes an ideal for human flourishing rather than something that can be measured and technically guided following a standard. In Eisnerian vocabulary, growth must be evaluated, and this requires a form of aesthetic/pedagogical connoisseurship (see also Väkevä 2019).

As was the case with *Bildung*, at first sight, this view of growth does not appear to align with posthumanism's understanding of human agency as intertwined with other forms of agencies in the actor-networks that produce meaning as mattering. When growth is associated only with human flourishing, it seems to connect to the humanist concept of *Bildung*, understood as a process where only humans support each other's growth (Väkevä 2012). Yet in his later works, Dewey also emphasized the continuity between different levels (or 'plateaus') of life, suggesting that growth could be witnessed as an ontological trait of all nature, evolving through transactions that create new systemic possibilities for meaning-making (see, e.g., Dewey 1996e). Through a posthumanist lens that recognizes the semiotic potential of all intra-actions, we need not confine growth to the parameters of human *Bildung*. In this view, machine systems can perhaps grow just as human systems do, as far as they coordinate with other actors to develop new ways to perform meaning. However, such systems cannot achieve cultivation in ways that satisfy the requirements of *Bildung* if they lack the capacity for *Sittlichkeit* or the ability to lead an ethical life. Thus, they can grow but not educate—or be educated.

Someday, AI systems may evolve to a plateau where they actively participate in the value frameworks of human societies in ways that justify their recognition as ethical agents. This raises questions about the criteria for such recognition: should it be based on their functional capabilities, such as a capability of decision-making that aligns with ethical norms, or on their ability to demonstrate reflective consciousness? Within AI ethics, this debate often focuses on whether the mere appearance of reflective capacity in AI models is sufficient to grant them ethical rights or whether more intrinsic signs of sentience will be required. This relates to the so-called *alignment problem*, which encourages us to ask whether the operation of AI can be adjusted to human needs and what happens if it begins to construct its own goals (see, e.g., Coeckelbergh 2020; Gibert and Martin 2022; Gordon and Pasvenskiene 2021). Some commentators caution against anthropomorphizing AI based on surface-level behaviors, projecting capabilities into it that we might wish it to have (Cecchini et al. 2024; Placani 2024). In contrast, others argue that if AI models exhibit moral traits, denying them ethical consideration might reflect a bias rather than a justified stance, at least when judged from a pragmatic standpoint (see, e.g., Gilbert et al. 2023; Harris and Anthis 2021; Ladak et al. 2024; Wilks 2010). This discussion touches on broader philosophical issues, including the nature of rights, the criteria for recognizing moral agency, and the boundaries of anthropocentric ethics in an increasingly technologically integrated world.

One could also maintain that in aesthetic contexts, AI already manifests value-based agency. This might be particularly true for GenAI, which can be maybe even described as an artist, even if it is not capable of experiencing anything aesthetically. After all, GenAI can perform aesthetic effects and outcomes by generating artistic content. However, one can claim that this artistic agency does not qualify as an educational agency. This claim would be based on the premise that educational agency requires more than an ability to perform in a seemingly appropriate manner in specific domains of action—namely, the generic capability of ethical deliberation, which one develops in touch with other ethical agents as part of *Bildung*. AI's inability to make ethical judgments means it cannot guide situations toward ethical outcomes without human involvement. Human teachers, acting in the role of educators, must thus be the judges of the qualitative transformation that education, at best, enacts. This would also seem to be the conclusion toward which educational aesthetics guides us: one needs to experience situations aesthetically in order to realize their full value potential. Such realization of the aesthetic potential requires the capability of aesthetic judgment, which is also a requirement for educational criticism.

Another way to put this is that even if GenAI would gain pedagogical agency as an instructor or a teacher, it cannot develop the pedagogical tact required from an educator as long as it lacks the capacity to experience situations as ethically and aesthetically value invested. As portrayed by Max van Manen (1991, 2015), pedagogical tact encompasses contextual understanding and responsiveness that good educators demonstrate when interacting with students in pedagogical situations. This concept of tact emphasizes three key elements: sensitivity, the courage to improvise when circumstances change, and ethical consideration toward turning teaching into praxis—or, put differently, it emphasizes phronesis, a contextual capacity to act appropriately in variable circumstances. In this framework, pedagogical praxis incorporates tact as phronesis through the implementation of ethical choices in situ. The core argument here is that pedagogical situations are too complex for algorithmic systems, even self-adapting ones, to grasp their nuances fully. When machine agency becomes an element of learning environments, these situations become even more intricate, with an increased need for pedagogical tact.

References

Alexander Mordvintsev. 2024. https://www.lerandom.art/artists/alexander-mordvintsev.

Audry, Sofian. 2021. *Art in the Age of Learning Machines*. Cambridge, MA: The MIT Press.

Augustsson, Gunnar, and Lena Boström. 2016. Teachers' Leadership in the Didactic Room: A Systematic Literature Review of International Research. *Acta Didactica Norge* 10 (3): 7. https://doi.org/10.5617/adno.2883.

Berry, David M., and Michael Dieter, eds. 2015. *Postdigital Aesthetics*. London: Palgrave Macmillan UK. https://doi.org/10.1057/9781137437204.

Bozkurt, Aras. 2023. Unleashing the Potential of Generative AI, Conversational Agents and Chatbots in Educational Praxis: A Systematic Review and Bibliometric Analysis of GenAI in Education. *Open Praxis* 15 (4): 261–270. https://doi.org/10.55982/openpraxis.15.4.609.

Cecchini, Dario, Michael Pflanzer, and Veljko Dubljević. 2024. Aligning Artificial Intelligence with Moral Intuitions: An Intuitionist Approach to the Alignment Problem. *AI Ethics*. https://doi.org/10.1007/s43681-024-00496-5.

Chang, Minsuk, Stefania Druga, Alex Fiannaca, Pedro Vergani, Chinmay Kulkarni, Carrie Cai, and Michael Terry. 2023. The Prompt Artists. https://doi.org/10.48550/ARXIV.2303.12253.

Coeckelbergh, Mark. 2020. *AI Ethics*. Cambridge, MA: The MIT press.

Dasari, Dadan, Agus Hendriyanto, Sani Sahara, Didi Suryadi, Lukman H. Muhaimin, Theodore Chao, and Laila Fitriana. 2024. ChatGPT in Didactical Tetrahedron, Does It Make an Exception? A Case Study in Mathematics Teaching and Learning. *Frontiers in Education* 8:1295413. https://doi.org/10.3389/feduc.2023.1295413.

Dewey, John. 1996a. *The Collected Works of John Dewey, 1882–1953 (2nd release). Electronic edition. The Later Works of John Dewey, 1925–1953. The Middle Works of John Dewey, 1899–1924. Volume 9: 1916, Democracy and Education*. Carbondale and Edwardsville, IL/Charlottesville, VA: Southern Illinois University Press/InteLex.

Dewey, John. 1996e. *The Collected Works of John Dewey, 1882–1953 (2nd release). Electronic edition. The Later Works of John Dewey, 1925–1953. The Later Works of John Dewey, 1925–1953. Volume 12: 1938, Logic: The Theory of Inquiry*. Carbondale and Edwardsville, IL/Charlottesville, VA: Southern Illinois University Press/InteLex.

Elgammal, Ahmed, Bingchen Liu, Mohamed Elhoseiny, and Marian Mazzone. 2017. CAN: Creative Adversarial Networks, Generating "Art" by Learning About Styles and Deviating from Style Norms. https://doi.org/10.48550/ARXIV.1706.07068.

Gao, Didei, Lei Ji, Luowei Zhou, Kevin Q. Lin, Joya Chen, Zihan Fan, and Mike Z. Shou. 2023. AssistGPT: A General Multi-modal Assistant That Can Plan, Execute, Inspect, and Learn. https://doi.org/10.48550/ARXIV.2306.08640.

Gates, Bill. 2023. The Age of AI Has Begun. *GatesNotes*, 21 March. https://www.gatesnotes.com/The-Age-of-AI-Has-Begun.

Gibert, Martin, and Dominic Martin. 2022. In Search of the Moral Status of AI: Why Sentience Is a Strong Argument. *AI & Society* 37 (1): 319–330. https://doi.org/10.1007/s00146-021-01179-z.

Gilbert, Thomas K., Megan W. Brozek, and Andrew Brozek. 2023. Beyond Bias and Compliance: Towards Individual Agency and Plurality of Ethics in AI. https://doi.org/10.48550/ARXIV.2302.12149.

Goodchild, Simon, and Bharath Sriraman. 2012. Revisiting the Didactic Triangle: From the Particular to the General. *ZDM* 44 (5): 581–585. https://doi.org/10.1007/s11858-012-0449-3.

Gordon, John-Stewart, and Ausrine Pasvenskiene. 2021. Human Rights for Robots? A Literature Review. *AI and Ethics* 1 (4): 579–591. https://doi.org/10.1007/s43681-021-00050-7.

Harris, Jamie, and Jacy R. Anthis. 2021. The Moral Consideration of Artificial Entities: A Literature Review. *Science and Engineering Ethics* 27:53. https://doi.org/10.1007/s11948-021-00331-8.

Hutson, James, and Peter Cotroneo. 2023. Generative AI Tools in Art Education: Exploring Prompt Engineering and Iterative Processes for Enhanced Creativity. *Metaverse* 4 (1): 1–14. https://doi.org/10.54517/m.v4i1.2164.

Knox, Jeremy. 2019. What Does the 'Postdigital' Mean for Education? Three Critical Perspectives on the Digital, with Implications for Educational Research and Practice. *Postdigital Science and Education* 1 (2): 357–370. https://doi.org/10.1007/s42438-019-00045-y.

Ladak, Ali, Jamie Harris, and Jacy R. Anthis. 2024. Which Artificial Intelligences Do People Care About Most? A Conjoint Experiment on Moral Consideration. https://doi.org/10.48550/ARXIV.2403.09405.

Miller, Arthur I. 2019. *The Artist in the Machine: The World of AI-Powered Creativity*. Cambridge, MA: The MIT Press.

Mills, Kathy A., and Len Unsworth. 2017. Multimodal Literacy. In *Oxford Research Encyclopedia of Education*, ed. K.A. Mills and L. Unsworth. Oxford: Oxford University Press. https://doi.org/10.1093/acrefore/9780190264093.013.232.

Mills, Kelly, Pati Ruiz, Keun-woo Lee, Merjike Coenraad, Judi Fusco, Jeremy Roschelle, and Josh Weisgrau. 2024. AI Literacy: A Framework to Understand, Evaluate, and Use Emerging Technology. *Digital Promise*. https://doi.org/10.51388/20.500.12265/218.

Ng, Davy T. K., Jac K. L. Leung, Samuel K. W. Chu, and Maggie S. Qiao. 2021. Conceptualizing AI Literacy: An Exploratory Review. *Computers and Education: Artificial Intelligence* 2:100041. https://doi.org/10.1016/j.caeai.2021.100041.

Pinski, Marc, and Alexander Benlian. 2024. AI Literacy for Users—A Comprehensive Review and Future Research Directions of Learning Methods, Components, and Effects. *Computers in Human Behavior: Artificial Humans* 2 (1): 100062. https://doi.org/10.1016/j.chbah.2024.100062.

Placani, Adriana. 2024. Anthropomorphism in AI: Hype and Fallacy. *AI and Ethics* 4 (3): 691–698. https://doi.org/10.1007/s43681-024-00419-4.

Ploin, Anne, Rebecca Eyonon, Isis Hjorth, and Michael A. Osborne. 2024. *AI and the Arts: How Machine Learning Is Changing Artistic Work. Report from the Creative Algorithmic Intelligence Research Project.* Oxford: University of Oxford. https://www.oii.ox.ac.uk/wp-content/uploads/2022/03/040222-AI-and-the-Arts_FINAL.pdf.

Rancière, Jacques. 2012. *Aisthesis: Scenes from the Aesthetic Regime of Art.* London: Verso.

Rezat, Sebastian, and Rudolf Sträßer. 2012. From the Didactical Triangle to the Socio-Didactical Tetrahedron: Artifacts as Fundamental Constituents of the Didactical Situation. *ZDM* 44 (5): 641–651. https://doi.org/10.1007/s11858-012-0448-4.

Ruthven, Kenneth. 2012. The Didactical Tetrahedron as a Heuristic for Analysing the Incorporation of Digital Technologies Into Classroom Practice in Support of Investigative Approaches to Teaching Mathematics. *ZDM* 44 (5): 627–640. https://doi.org/10.1007/s11858-011-0376-8.

Salonen, Arto O., and Marjatta Brady. 2015. Ekososiaalinen sivistys herättää luottamusta tulevaisuuteen [Ecosocial *Bildung* Raises Trust in the Future]. *Aikuiskasvatus* 35 (1): 4–15. https://doi.org/10.33336/aik.94118.

Tall, David. 1986. Using the Computer as an Environment for Building and Testing Mathematical Concepts. In *Intelligence, Learning and Understanding in Mathematics: A Tribute to Richard Skemp*, ed. David Tall and Michael Thomas, 21–36. Post Pressed.

Tavin, Kevin, Gila Kolb, and Juuso Tervo, ed. 2021. *Post-Digital, Post-Internet Art and Education: The Future is All-Over.* Cham: Springer.

Väkevä, Lauri. 2012. Experiencing Growth as a Natural Phenomenon: John Dewey's Philosophy and the Bildung Tradition. In *Theories of Bildung and Growth*, ed. Pauli Siljader, Ari Kivelä, and Ari Sutinen, 261–279. Rotterdam: Sense.

Väkevä, Lauri. 2019. Evaluation for Equality: Applying a Classical Pragmatist Perspective in Qualitative Assessment in Finnish General Music Education. In *The Oxford Handbook of Philosophical and Qualitative Assessment in Music Education*, ed. David J. Elliott, Marissa Silverman, and Gary E. McPherson, 100–121. New York, NY: Oxford University Press. https://doi.org/10.1093/oxfordhb/9780190265182.013.7.

Väkevä, Lauri, and Heidi Partti. 2025 (in print). Towards AI Didactics: Call for Teachers to Train Large Language Models for Research Writing in Higher Arts Education. In *Education and Artificial Intelligence Handbook*, ed. Guy Tchibozo. Cham: Springer.

Van Manen, Max. 1991. *The Tact of Teaching: The Meaning of Pedagogical Thoughtfulness.* Albany, NY: State University of New York Press.

Van Manen, Max. 2015. *Pedagogical tact: Knowing What to Do When You Don't Know What to Do.* Milton Park: Routledge.

Wiesner, Christian, Kerstin Zechner, and Simone Breit. 2023. The Didactic Triangle from Sign-Theoretical Perspectives to Deepen the Pedagogical Situation. A paper at *ECER 2023* Conference, 22 August. https://eera-ecer.de/ecer-programmes/conference/28/contribution/57908.

Wilks, Yorick, ed. 2010. *Close Engagements with Artificial Companions: Key Social, Psychological, Ethical and Design Issues.* Amsterdam: John Benjamins Publishing Company.

CHAPTER 7

Empowering Machine Voices: The Hybrid Temporalities of AI Art

Abstract This chapter explores artistic AI agency through the lens of temporality. Voice is again used as a metaphor to consider how to maintain empowered expression in polytemporal and, therefore, polysemiotic human-GenAI entanglements. The chapter also includes a section discussing the possibility of AI art without corporeal embodiment.

Keywords Artificial intelligence • Agency • Temporality • Digitality • AI art

One approach to understanding human and AI agencies in art(s) education is to examine their distinct operational modes. This chapter explores these agencies through the lens of temporality. Voice serves again as a metaphor to consider how to maintain empowered expression in polytemporal and, thus, polysemiotic, human-machine collaborations. The question of the indispensability of corporality arises as the interpenetration of computer and human bodies is examined in a shared aesthetic space conducive to art(s) education.

Sonic Temporalities of Digital Technology

Wolfgang Ernst (2013) argues that digital machines and humans handle time in fundamentally different ways, affecting how these machines operate in creative contexts. Unlike humans, digital machines exhibit a

L. Väkevä, *Voicing Responsible AI Pedagogy for Music and Visual Arts Education*, https://doi.org/10.1007/978-3-031-86410-0_7

non-linear sense of time, which Ernst (29–31) defines as "tempor(e)ality." There is also an artistic dimension in this characterization: Ernst (ibid. 31, 144, 2016) elaborates on the concept through "tonality" and "sonicity," describing how tempor(e)ality is embedded non-linearly in digital infrastructures, transforming our conventional understanding of time as a sequence of moments. Building on Ernst's work, Shintaro Miyazaki (2012, 244) characterizes the tempor(e)ality of digital technology as consisting of "algorhythmic" events—"time-based, technological processes, which occur when matter is modulated by symbolic and logical structures." Though these events typically operate beyond our perceptual threshold, they become particularly noticeable and influential when the technologies malfunction or otherwise act surprisingly (ibid.).

Digital technology's non-linear nature also challenges our traditional view of knowledge as representation (see also Barker 2012). Ernst (2013) argues that in the material processes of sonicity, sign(al)s break free from linear temporal constraints to become polytemporal, constantly available for recall and reuse, like voices without reference. Digital sonicities flow freely through media channels, open to new semiotic interpretations across different contexts. This free-form, multidirectional, and multitemporal (or "thick"; see Barker 2012) digital processing creates semiotic spaces where human and algorithmic performativities intersect, producing a synchronous rather than narrative sense of time. Thus, when engaging with digital technology, we enter new relationships within actor-networks that are liberated from the need to represent reality at a fixed moment.

Following Ernst (2013), traditional linear narrative structures cannot fully capture the essence of digital creativity, as the latter transcends conventional representational frameworks. Digital machines operate in a distinctly non-human temporal mode that humans can comprehend only in retrospect but, allegedly, can experience aesthetically through art (Barker 2012). Given this understanding, expecting human-like projectivity from these machines may be futile, as their intentional capacities follow a different logic, namely, one that aligns more closely with polysemiotic artistic expression. This perspective particularly suits viewing GenAI as a performative technology, helping identify its unique poietic mode of operation. In this framework, GenAI's voicings emerge as both polytemporal and polysemiotic, inviting human artists and audiences to engage in its performativity in its own terms.

The Aesthetic Polytemporality of GenAI

Another perspective on the distinction between human and AI agency emerges when one considers that aesthetic qualities inherent to human experience appear absent in algorithmic processes. When discussing machine learning-based art, Audry (2021) observes that traditional adaptive AI systems mainly follow a computational dogma based on formal, rule-based logic. Audry (ibid.) then contrasts these first-order systems with the second-order dynamics of newer self-adaptive AI. This self-adaptivity goes beyond simply performing better within pre-programmed parameters; it involves producing novelty. In their perpetual search for new action patterns, machine learning systems can generate new aesthetic situations and demonstrate new forms of creativity—and, thus, ostensibly, create new art.

Audry (ibid.) posits that such second-order technological systems herald new aesthetic spaces that can be explored through cooperation between human and machine actors. In line with this, Barker (2012, 3) describes the intervention of digital technology into aesthetic spaces as having the power to alter "our sensory understanding of the world" and, thus, our aesthetic experience. Such altering of the sensible (in Rancièrian terms) does not take place primarily through the use of technologies to solve epistemic problems. Instead, human and machine agencies entangle in and interpenetrate an aesthetic space to compose new configurations of mattering where the linear reference between a sign and what it refers to is troubled by polytemporal webs of meaning. In such conditions, it might make sense to think of aesthetic spaces as distributed between human and machine agencies.

The possibility of the emergence of aesthetic experience in human-AI entanglements deserves attention from art(s) educators. The latter should be able to make pedagogically sustainable judgments about how GenAI and other self-adapting technologies become "involved" or "interested" in configuring shared aesthetic spaces through "interpenetration of the [computer and human] bodies" (26, 98, 109). Even if our perceptions can be constantly "remade and reordered" through our entanglements with digital temporalities (ibid.), pedagogical tact is still essential for helping the students to make sense of this "techno-aesthetic process" (191).

Does an Artist's Voice Require a Body?

The intertwining of human and machine bodies might lead one's imagination astray from the realities of current GenAI to the sci-fi narratives of human-like robots. However, embedding AI in an android body is not a requisite for human-machine artistic collaborations. As discussed above, it makes sense to examine AI art as an entanglement of material processes of mattering and to grant AI agency in the actor-networks that reconfigure aesthetic spaces through performative acts. Indeed, together, Deweyan pragmatist and Baradian posthumanist perspectives encourage us to think of *all* bodies as agentive assemblages of intra-active processes that, under certain conditions, bring about transactional changes, leading to transformations and new distributions of the sensible.

Following this lead in art(s) education, one might ask how pedagogical interaction supports the conditions of such transactions and, thus, leads to the artistic growth of the students. Above, it has been argued that pedagogical support is educative only to the degree that it supports *Bildung*, viz., a lifelong process of becoming an agent capable of acting ethically in cultural and social milieux. In this outlook, the transformations enacted through pedagogical decisions produce social bodies—bodies that are motivated to find meaning together.

What about GenAI? Can it develop a social body? This question might be premature. Instead, we should maybe ask under what conditions it can participate in actor-networks that bring about systemic changes, heeding future possibilities of action. Perhaps the 'body' need not be understood as a material center of sensory focus but rather a distributed and expansive assemblage of intra-active processes that, under certain conditions, create a sense of being an intentional agent aimed at actualizing potential changes in the lifeworld. When digitality enters the picture, such assemblages harness the potential of multitemporal sonicity, allowing signifiers to float freely and to seek references from a vast web of possible interpretants through various kinds of voicings. This sonicity allegedly creates a dynamic tension between past, present, and future—a tension that Dewey (1996e) also located as the heart of inquiry, which he saw as a mediating between different temporalities. In other words, digitality enhances the organic body's functions to seek meanings through multiple channels, transcending (and also perhaps transgressing) time and space. Thus, it also provides new possibilities for artistic inquiries.

Following Barker (2012, 30), one could also think about bodies as accumulations of solutions to bygone problems, that is, cumulated storages of information ready to be interpreted as knowledge when the occasion calls. In this sense, bodies present themselves as organic hubs of information technology, and it makes little sense to draw functional distinctions between their natural and artificial origins when considering their effectiveness as such technologies. When human and digital bodies converge, the possibilities of information technology claim an immensely broader semiotic space due to the emancipation of time and place as determinants of meaning. The "digital encounter" (31) thus dramatically expands our naturally evolved capabilities, providing information that is no longer dependent on location and occasion. Such expanded virtual capabilities were already anticipated by transhumanists, who recognized how rapid technological innovation is rapidly changing our understanding of human potential (More 1990). The cyborg identity heralded by Haraway (1991) has become a reality not just through the added capabilities of human enhancement but also, perhaps more significantly, through the coordinated action between humans and AI.

What of art, then? Does not an artist need an organic body? The above discussion has tried to argue that when considered from the philosophical standpoints of Deweyan pragmatism and Baradian posthumanism and theoretically examined through the lens of actor-network theory, art is also possible in human-machine entanglements—and maybe even in entanglements that do not include human bodies. When machines develop autonomy in decision-making and generate outcomes that can be interpreted as significant in specific contexts of action, they also establish creative agency. Contemporary digital art provides ample possibilities to study how such autonomy shifts the coordinates of aesthetic spaces, redistributing the realm of the sensible through the sonic options of digital tempor(e)ality. Such redistribution of the aesthetic space and time does not require that all participating actors are capable of experiencing these spaces in the way humans and other natural organisms do. However, they need the capability to *perform meaningfully* by making things happen in ways that make a difference in the lifeworld(s) of the sensing beings. Yet, the judgment of what constitutes art—the aesthetic judgment—cannot be purely algorithmic if one expects art's value to relate to how it can be experienced. If we follow Dewey and the proponents of educational aesthetics, experiencing art is based on an ability to make qualitative judgments of value, which seem to be out of the reach of the present AI. While such judgments might not require a human body, we do not yet have other material means for it. Thus, AI art requires a human element to realize its aesthetic potential. It is the continuing task of the art(s) educators to help us build our capabilities to make it do so.

References

Audry, Sofian. 2021. *Art in the Age of Learning Machines.* Cambridge, MA: The MIT Press.

Barker, Timothy S. 2012. *Time and the Digital: Connecting Technology, Aesthetics, and a Process Philosophy of Time.* Chicago, IL: Chicago University Press.

Dewey, John. 1996e. *The Collected Works of John Dewey, 1882–1953 (2nd release). Electronic edition. The Later Works of John Dewey, 1925–1953. The Later Works of John Dewey, 1925–1953. Volume 12: 1938, Logic: The Theory of Inquiry.* Carbondale and Edwardsville, IL/Charlottesville, VA: Southern Illinois University Press/InteLex.

Ernst, Wolfgang. 2013. *Digital Memory and the Archive.* Minneapolis, MN: University of Minnesota Press.

———. 2016. *Sonic Time Machines: Explicit Sound, Sirenic Voices, and Implicit Sonicity.* Amsterdam: Amsterdam University Press.

Haraway, Donna J. 1991. A Cyborg Manifesto: Science, Technology, and Socialist-Feminism in the Late Twentieth Century. In *Simians, Cyborgs and Women: The Reinvention of Nature,* 149–182. New York, NY: Routledge.

Miyazaki, Shintaro. 2012. Algorhythmics: Understanding Micro-Temporality in Computational Cultures. *Computational Culture* 2. http://computationalculture.net/algorhythmics-understanding-micro-temporality-in-computational-cultures/.

More, Max. 1990. Transhumanism: Towards a Futuristic Philosophy. https://www.ildodopensiero.it/wp-content/uploads/2019/03/max-more-transhumanism-towards-a-futurist-philosophy.pdf.

CHAPTER 8

Conclusion

Abstract This chapter concludes the previous discussion by providing a short recap and considering its possible implications. The chapter considers explicitly what we can expect from GenAI in the near future in aesthetic terms and how we can make it a part of pedagogically sustainable art(s) education.

Keywords Artificial intelligence • Art education • Aesthetics • Sustainability • Pedagogy

This book has discussed the relationship between GenAI and art(s) education from the perspective of voicing, emphasizing a pedagogical angle and focusing especially on visual and auditory arts. Now, it is time to conclude and consider the possibilities this discussion might instigate. Before that, a short recap might be in order.

The introduction clarified some key concepts and established a philosophical framework based on Deweyan pragmatism and Baradian posthumanism, which were suggested as a shared conceptual ground for the main argumentation of the book. Combined with actor-network theory, these approaches indicate an ontology that embraces a holistic and pluralist view of the world as a network of mattering processes based on entangled intra-actions. Under certain conditions, intra-actions enact

L. Väkevä, *Voicing Responsible AI Pedagogy for Music and Visual Arts Education*, https://doi.org/10.1007/978-3-031-86410-0_8

transactions, introducing new systemic levels of organization and, thus, new habits of action. This process ontology also acknowledges the symmetrical roles of human and non-human (or more-than-human) agencies in creating meaning in situations where semiotic actors find themselves. From this perspective, GenAI can be regarded as a collaborator in performative acts that help us understand our entanglements.

Voicing provided both a practical case and a key metaphor for the ensuing discussion of the possibilities and challenges of GenAI in art(s) education. Voice cloning was also discussed as an example of how GenAI may change our relationship with digital technology, suggesting a future where human-like AI may no more be perceived as uncanny but, instead, accepted as having an equal voice in transactions that redistribute 'the sensible.' The potential impact of GenAI on redistributing aesthetic spaces was also recognized, followed by an analysis of sustainability issues surrounding the use of GenAI in pedagogical and other contexts. These two approaches were then used as a basis for a pragmatist/posthumanist reading of the need to develop critical AI literacy to support sustainable pedagogies in and between the arts.

The book then reviewed the aesthetic potential of multimodal GenAI, proposing a transdisciplinary approach to studying its impact on the arts and art(s) education. It also examined the creative capabilities of GenAI in relation to traditional didactic approaches to teaching, proposing an optional way to conceptualize how such adaptive technologies can engage in the relationship between teaching, learning, and subject matter. It was concluded that while AI can learn, instruct, and perhaps even grow, it cannot educate because it lacks the capacity for ethical deliberation. Therefore, a tactful human teacher is still essential for art(s) education that aims to foster *Bildung*.

After exploring how GenAI potentially disrupts traditional aesthetic approaches to education within and across the arts, the book proceeded to discuss the unique polytemporality that digital technology—and particularly GenAI—introduces to artistic practices, making us aware of the polysemiotic aesthetic potential of the human-machine entanglements. While unfolding such aesthetic potential may well require working with the machines rather than merely using them as tools, it was still maintained that human experience is the only available criterion for perceiving such potential. Combined with the premise that humans are needed to educate humans toward *Bildung*, this perspective suggests that art(s) educators need to understand how GenAI generates artistic content and what kinds of aesthetic possibilities are implied.

Looking ahead, it seems unavoidable that the rapid advancement of GenAI, especially with the development of MLLMs, holds promise to transform art(s) education. These models, which can seamlessly synthesize and convert various data modalities, are set to provide new opportunities for creative expression and transdisciplinary learning and even to introduce new artistic disciplines, expanding the possibilities of artistic growth.

However, the transformative potential of GenAI also comes with challenges. Its incorporation into art(s) education must consider the ethical, social, cultural, political, economic, and aesthetic implications of relying on increasingly autonomous technological systems. Other forms of sustainability must be recognized as relevant when evaluating the pedagogical sustainability of using GenAI in art(s) classes.

Multimodal GenAI further raises philosophical questions about authorship, originality, and the boundaries of human creativity. Allegedly, as these systems learn to 'voice' in the aesthetic idioms of various artistic disciplines, there is a risk of homogenizing artistic expression, which could dilute the qualitative uniqueness that arguably is central to both contemporary art and aesthetic experience. Such homogenization seems to be antithetical to the connoisseurship that ought to be a foundational part of a balanced education in the arts and beyond. To address these challenges, art(s) educators should strive to cultivate critical AI literacy, empowering students to interrogate the affordances embedded in these technologies and in how they interpenetrate late modern life.

Art(s) educators should also embrace GenAI as a collaborator rather than a replacement, encouraging students to engage with it experimentally and showing leadership in guiding it along with the students. By nurturing reflective practices of AI use and promoting an understanding of the complex entanglements between humans, technologies, and the environments they inhabit together, art(s) educators can confirm that GenAI expands, rather than curbs, the aesthetic space. However, integrating GenAI into art(s) education also demands a careful balancing act: embracing its capacity to transform the aesthetic realm of the sensible while remaining alert to its algorithmic potential to limit artistic freedom. It can be argued that this balancing is especially critical in the late modern culture, in which art is constantly in danger of becoming a commodity in service of individual performativity.

References

Abrams, Zara. 2023. AI Is Changing Every Aspect of Psychology. Here's What to Watch for. *Monitor on Psychology* 54 (5): 46. https://www.apa.org/monitor/2023/07/psychology-embracing-ai.

Alexander Mordvintsev. 2024. https://www.lerandom.art/artists/alexander-mordvintsev.

Alexander, Thomas M. 1987. *John Dewey's Theory of Art, Experience, and Nature: The Horizons of Feeling*. Albany, NY: State University of New York Press.

Allen, Aaron S. 2019. Aesthetics and Sustainability. In *Encyclopedia of Sustainability in Higher Education*, ed. Walter Leal Filho, 25–33. Cham: Springer. https://doi.org/10.1007/978-3-030-11352-0_403.

Allyn, Bobby. 2024. Scarlett Johansson Says She Is "Shocked, Angered" Over New ChatGPT Voice. *Npr*, 20 May. https://www.npr.org/2024/05/20/1252495087/openai-pulls-ai-voice-that-was-compared-to-scarlett-johansson-in-the-movie-her.

Amnesty. 2022. The Social Atrocity: Meta and the Right to Remedy for the Rohingya. https://www.amnesty.org/en/documents/ASA16/5933/2022/en/.

Anthropic. 2024. 'Hume AI Creates Emotionally Intelligent Voice Interactions with Claude. https://www.anthropic.com/customers/hume.

Arendt, Hannah. 1989. *The Human Condition*. Chicago, IL: University of Chicago Press.

Audry, Sofian. 2021. *Art in the Age of Learning Machines*. Cambridge, MA: The MIT Press.

L. Väkevä, *Voicing Responsible AI Pedagogy for Music and Visual Arts Education*, https://doi.org/10.1007/978-3-031-86410-0

Augustsson, Gunnar, and Lena Boström. 2016. Teachers' Leadership in the Didactic Room: A Systematic Literature Review of International Research. *Acta Didactica Norge* 10 (3): 7. https://doi.org/10.5617/adno.2883.

Austin, John L. 2009. *How to Do Things with Words: The William James Lectures Delivered at Harvard University in 1955.* Cambridge, MA: Harvard University Press.

Bakhtin, Mikhail M. 1983. *The Dialogic Imagination: Four Essays by M. M. Bakhtin.* Austin, TX: University of Texas Press.

Barad, Karen. 2003. Posthumanist Performativity: Toward an Understanding of How Matter Comes to Matter. *Signs: Journal of Women in Culture and Society* 28 (3): 801–831. https://doi.org/10.1086/345321.

———. 2006. *Meeting the Universe Halfway: Quantum Physics and the Entanglement of Matter and Meaning.* Durham, NC: Duke University Press. https://doi.org/10.1215/9780822388128.

Barker, Timothy S. 2012. *Time and the Digital: Connecting Technology, Aesthetics, and a Process Philosophy of Time.* Chicago, IL: Chicago University Press.

Barrett, Margaret S., Andrea Creech, and Katie Zhukov. 2021. Creative Collaboration and Collaborative Creativity: A Systematic Literature Review. *Frontiers in Psychology* 12:713445. https://doi.org/10.3389/fpsyg.2021.713445.

Barrington, Sarah, and Hany Farid. 2024. People Are Poorly Equipped to Detect AI-Powered Voice Clones. http://arxiv.org/abs/2410.03791.

Bauman, Zygmunt. 2000. *Liquid Modernity.* Cambridge: Polity.

Baxter, Lesile A., ed. 2011. *Voicing Relationships: A Dialogic Perspective.* Thousand Oaks, CA: Sage.

Beck, Ulrich. 1992. *Risk Society: Towards a New Modernity.* Thousand Oaks, CA: Sage.

Bell, Daniel. 1976. The Coming of the Post-Industrial Society. *The Educational Forum* 40 (4): 574–579. https://doi.org/10.1080/00131727609336501.

Bender, Emily M., Timnit Gebru, Angelina McMillan-Major, and Schmargaret Shmitchell. 2021. On the Dangers of Stochastic Parrots: Can Language Models Be Too Big? In *Proceedings of the 2021 ACM Conference on Fairness, Accountability, and Transparency, Virtual Event*, 610–623. New York, NY: Association of for Computing Machinery. https://doi.org/10.1145/3442188.3445922.

Benjamin, Walter. 1996. The Work of Art in the Age of Mechanical Reproduction. In *Selected Writings. Volume 3: 1935—1938*, ed. Howard Eiland and Michael W. Jennings, 101–133. Cambridge, MA: Belknap.

Bentz, Julia, Leticia Do Carmo, Nicole Schafenacker, Jörn Schirok, and Sara D. Corso. 2022. Creative, Embodied Practices, and the Potentialities for Sustainability Transformations. *Sustainability Science* 17 (2): 687–699. https://doi.org/10.1007/s11625-021-01000-2.

Berry, David M., and Michael Dieter, eds. 2015. *Postdigital Aesthetics*. London: Palgrave Macmillan UK. https://doi.org/10.1057/9781137437204.

Beville, Maria. 2009. *Gothic-Postmodernism: Voicing the Terrors of Postmodernity*. Amsterdam: Rodopi. https://doi.org/10.1163/9789042026650.

Biesta, Gert. 2018. *Letting Art Teach. Art Education 'After' Joseph Beuys*. Arnhem: ArtEZ Press.

———. 2022. *World-Centred Education: A View for the Present*. London: Routledge.

Bleher, Hannah, and Matthias Braun. 2023. Reflections on Putting AI Ethics into Practice: How Three AI Ethics Approaches Conceptualize Theory and Practice. *Science and Engineering Ethics* 29 (3): 21. https://doi.org/10.1007/s11948-023-00443-3.

Boddington, Paula. 2023. *AI Ethics: A Textbook*. Singapore: Springer. https://doi.org/10.1007/978 981-19-9382-4.

Boisvert, Raymond D. 1988. *Dewey's Metaphysics*. New York, NY: Fordham University Press.

Borrows, John, and Kent McNeil, eds. 2022. *Voicing Identity: Cultural Appropriation and Indigenous Issues*. Toronto: University of Toronto Press.

Bostrom, Nick. 2014. *Superintelligence: Paths, Dangers, Strategies*. New York, NY: Oxford University Press.

Boyer, Robert H. W., Nicole D. Peterson, Poonam Arora, and Kevin Caldwell. 2016. Five Approaches to Social Sustainability and an Integrated Way Forward. *Sustainability* 8 (9): 878. https://doi.org/10.3390/su8090878.

Bozkurt, Aras. 2023. Unleashing the Potential of Generative AI, Conversational Agents and Chatbots in Educational Praxis: A Systematic Review and Bibliometric Analysis of GenAI in Education. *Open Praxis* 15 (4): 261–270. https://doi.org/10.55982/openpraxis.15.4.609.

Braidotti, Rosi. 2002. *Metamorphoses: Towards a Materialist Theory of Becoming*. Cambridge: Polity.

Bray, Peter, and Oliver Bray, eds. 2013. *Voicing Trauma and Truth: Narratives of Disruption and Transformation*. Freeland: Inter-Disciplinary Press.

Bruhn, Siglind, ed. 2002. *Voicing the Ineffable: Musical Representations of Religious Experience*. Hillsdale, NY: Pendragon Press.

Buchler, Justus. 1990. *Metaphysics of Natural Complexes*. Albany, NY: State University of New York Press.

Butler, Judith. 1988. Performative Acts and Gender Constitution: An Essay in Phenomenology and Feminist Theory. *Theatre Journal* 40 (4): 519–531. https://doi.org/10.2307/3207893.

Callicott, J. Baird. 2018. Ecological Sustainability. In *A Sustainable Philosophy—The Work of Bryan Norton*, ed. Sahotra Sarkar and Ben A. Minteer, 27–47. Cham: Springer. https://doi.org/10.1007/978-3-319-92597-4_3.

Cappaletti, Gloria M. 2023. Unveiling AI Hallucinations: Exploring the Enigmatic Art of 20 Visionary AI Creators. *Red Eye*, 7 July. https://www.red-eye.world/c/unveiling-ai-hallucinations-exploring-the-enigmatic-art-of-20-visionary-ai-creators.

Carr, Wilfred, and Stephen Kemmis. 1986. *Becoming Critical: Education, Knowledge, and Action Research*. London: Routledge Falmer.

Cecchini, Dario, Michael Pflanzer, and Veljko Dubljević. 2024. Aligning Artificial Intelligence with Moral Intuitions: An Intuitionist Approach to the Alignment Problem. *AI Ethics*. https://doi.org/10.1007/s43681-024-00496-5.

Chalmers, David J. 2010. The Singularity: A Philosophical Analysis. *Journal of Consciousness Studies* 17 (9–10): 7–65.

Chan, Cecilia K. Y., and Katherine K. W. Lee. 2023. The AI Generation Gap: Are Gen Z Students More Interested in Adopting Generative AI Such as ChatGPT in Teaching and Learning Than Their Gen X and Millennial Generation Teachers? *Smart Learning Environments* 10 (1): 60. https://doi.org/10.1186/s40561-023-00269-3.

Chang, Minsuk, Stefania Druga, Alex Fiannaca, Pedro Vergani, Chinmay Kulkarni, Carrie Cai, and Michael Terry. 2023. The Prompt Artists. https://doi.org/10.48550/ARXIV.2303.12253.

Chen, Lin, Zhonghao Chen, Yubing Zhang, Yunfei Liu, Ahmed I. Osman, Mohamed Farghali, Jianmin Hua, Ahmed Al-Fatesh, Ikko Ihara, David W. Rooney, and Pow-Seng Yap. 2023. Artificial Intelligence-Based Solutions for Climate Change: A Review. *Environmental Chemistry Letters* 21 (5): 2525–2557. https://doi.org/10.1007/s10311-023-01617-y.

Chen, Min. 2024. French Collective Obvious Has Created an A.I. Art Generator That Can Read Your Mind. *Artnet*, 14 May. https://news.artnet.com/art-world/obvious-mind-to-image-ai-2486868.

Cheng, Mingyong, Xuexi Dang, and Zetao Yu. 2023. Fusion: Landscape and Beyond 2.0: An Interactive AI Generated Art Installation. *ACM SIGGRAPH Asia 2023 Art Gallery*, 1–2. https://doi.org/10.1145/3610537.3622954.

Clark, A. 2023. *The Experience Machine: How Our Minds Predict and Shape Reality*. London: Penguin Random House.

Clarke, Angela, and Shane Hulbert. 2016. Envisioning the Future: Working Toward Sustainability in Fine Art Education. *International Journal of Art & Design Education* 35 (1): 36–50. https://doi.org/10.1111/jade.12047.

Cochrane, Emily. 2024. Tennessee Makes A.I. an Outlaw to Protect Its Country Music and More. *The New York Times*, 21 March. https://www.nytimes.com/2024/03/21/us/politics/tennessee-ai-music-law.htm.

Coeckelbergh, Mark. 2020. *AI Ethics*. Cambridge, MA: The MIT press.

Collins, Nick, and Mick Grierson. 2024. Avoiding an AI-imposed Taylor's Version of All Music History. https://arxiv.org/abs/2402.14589v.

Coscarelli, Joe. 2023. Grimes Invited Anyone to Make A.I. Grimes Songs. Here Are Her Reviews. *The New York Times*, 24 May. https://www.nytimes.com/2023/05/24/arts/music/grimes-ai-songs.html.

Cotton, Kelsey, Katja De Vries, and Kivanc Tatar. 2024. Singing for the Missing: Bringing the Body Back to AI Voice and Speech Technologies. In *Proceedings of the 9th International Conference on Movement and Computing*, ed. Laura Karreman, 1–12. Association for Computing Machinery. https://doi.org/10.1145/3658852.3659065.

Creative Works Shape our Identity, Values, and Worldview. 2024. https://www.humanartistrycampaign.com/.

Danesi, Marcel. 2024. *AI-Generated Popular Culture: A Semiotic Perspective*. New York, NY: Palgrave Macmillan.

Dasari, Dadan, Agus Hendriyanto, Sani Sahara, Didi Suryadi, Lukman H. Muhaimin, Theodore Chao, and Laila Fitriana. 2024. ChatGPT in Didactical Tetrahedron, Does It Make an Exception? A Case Study in Mathematics Teaching and Learning. *Frontiers in Education* 8:1295413. https://doi.org/10.3389/feduc.2023.1295413.

Davis, Wes. 2024. Randy Travis Gets His Voice Back in a New Warner AI Music Experiment. *The Verge*, 6 May. https://www.theverge.com/2024/5/5/24149685/randy-travis-ai-voice-clone-song-where-that-came-from.

DeLanda, Manuel. 1995. The Geology of Morals—A Neomaterialist Interpretation. http://future-nonstop.org/c/818d3d85eca43d66ff0ebd1dfedda6e3.

Dellosa, Jeffrey T., and Eleonor C. Palconit. 2021. Artificial Intelligence (AI) in Renewable Energy Systems: A Condensed Review of Its Applications and Techniques. In *2021 IEEE International Conference on Environment and Electrical Engineering and 2021 IEEE Industrial and Commercial Power Systems Europe (EEEIC / I&CPS Europe)*, 1–6. https://doi.org/10.1109/EEEIC/ICPSEurope51590.2021.9584587.

Dewey, John. 1996a. *The Collected Works of John Dewey, 1882–1953 (2nd release). Electronic edition. The Later Works of John Dewey, 1925–1953. The Middle Works of John Dewey, 1899–1924. Volume 9: 1916, Democracy and Education*. Carbondale and Edwardsville, IL/Charlottesville, VA: Southern Illinois University Press/InteLex.

———. 1996b. *The Collected Works of John Dewey, 1882–1953 (2nd release). Electronic edition. The Later Works of John Dewey, 1925–1953. The Later Works of John Dewey, 1925–1953. Volume 4: 1929, The Quest for Certainty*. Carbondale and Edwardsville, IL/Charlottesville, VA: Southern Illinois University Press/InteLex.

———. 1996c. *The Collected Works of John Dewey, 1882–1953 (2nd release). Electronic edition. The Later Works of John Dewey, 1925–1953. Volume 1: 1925, Experience and Nature*. Carbondale and Edwardsville, IL/Charlottesville, VA: Southern Illinois University Press/InteLex.

———. 1996d. *The Collected Works of John Dewey, 1882–1953 (2nd release). Electronic edition. The Later Works of John Dewey, 1925–1953.* Volume 10: 1934, Art as Experience. Carbondale and Edwardsville, IL/Charlottesville, VA: Southern Illinois University Press/InteLex.

———. 1996e. *The Collected Works of John Dewey, 1882–1953 (2nd release). Electronic edition. The Later Works of John Dewey, 1925–1953. The Later Works of John Dewey, 1925–1953. Volume 12: 1938, Logic: The Theory of Inquiry.* Carbondale and Edwardsville, IL/Charlottesville, VA: Southern Illinois University Press/InteLex.

Dewey, John, and Arthur Bentley. 1996. Knowing and the Known. In *The Collected Works of John Dewey, 1882–1953 (2nd release). Electronic edition. The Later Works of John Dewey, 1925–1953. Volume 16: 1949–1952, Essays, Knowing and the Known*, 1–294. Carbondale and Edwardsville, IL/Charlottesville, VA: Southern Illinois University Press/InteLex.

Dewsbury, John-David. 2000. Performativity and the Event: Enacting a Philosophy of Difference. *Environment and Planning D: Society and Space* 18 (4): 473–496. https://doi.org/10.1068/d200t.

Diel, Alexander, and Michael Lewis. 2024. Deviation from Typical Organic Voices Best Explains a Vocal Uncanny Valley. *Computers in Human Behavior Reports* 14:100430. https://doi.org/10.1016/j.chbr.2024.100430.

Dillon, Teresa. 2003. Collaborating and Creating on Music Technologies. *International Journal of Educational Research* 39 (8): 893–897. https://doi.org/10.1016/j.ijer.2004.11.011.

Dolar, Mladen. 2006. *A Voice and Nothing More.* Cambridge, MA: MIT Press.

Dolphijn, Rick, and Iris V. D. Tuin. 2012. *New Materialism: Interviews & Cartographies.* London: Open Humanities Press. https://doi.org/10.3998/ohp.11515701.0001.001.

Duany, Andres, Elizabeth Plater-Zyberk, and Jeff Speck. 2001. *Suburban Nation: The Rise of Sprawl and the Decline of the American Dream.* New York, NY: Macmillan.

Edwards, Benj. 2023. Why ChatGPT and Bing Chat Are So Good at Making Things Up. A Look Inside the Hallucinating Artificial Minds of the Famous Text Prediction Bots. *Ars Technica*, 4 June. https://arstechnica.com/information-technology/2023/04/why-ai-chatbots-are-the-ultimate-bs-machines-and-how-people-hope-to-fix-them/.

Eisner, Elliot W. 1967. Educational Objectives: Help or Hindrance? *American Journal of Education* 91 (4): 549–560.

———. 1976. Educational Connoisseurship and Criticism: Their Form and Functions in Educational Evaluation. *Journal of Aesthetic Education* 10 (3/4): 135–150. https://doi.org/10.2307/3332067.

———. 2002. *The Arts and the Creation of Mind.* New Haven, CT: Yale University Press.

———. 2005. *Reimagining Schools: The Selected Works of Elliot W. Eisner.* New York, NY: Routledge.
———. 2017. *The Enlightened Eye: Qualitative Inquiry and the Enhancement of Educational Practice.* New York, NY: Teachers College Press.
Elgammal, Ahmed, Bingchen Liu, Mohamed Elhoseiny, and Marian Mazzone. 2017. CAN: Creative Adversarial Networks, Generating "Art" by Learning About Styles and Deviating from Style Norms. https://doi.org/10.48550/ARXIV.1706.07068.
Ernst, Wolfgang. 2013. *Digital Memory and the Archive.* Minneapolis, MN: University of Minnesota Press.
———. 2016. *Sonic Time Machines: Explicit Sound, Sirenic Voices, and Implicit Sonicity.* Amsterdam: Amsterdam University Press.
Fenwick, Tara, and Richard Edwards. 2013. Performative Ontologies: Sociomaterial Approaches to Researching Adult Education and Lifelong Learning. *European Journal for Research on the Education and Learning of Adults* 4 (1): 49–63. https://doi.org/10.3384/rela.2000-7426.rela0104.
Field, Hayden. 2024. OpenAI Pulls ChatGPT AI Voice Over Its Resemblance to Scarlett Johansson in the Movie 'Her'. *CNBC*, 20 May. https://www.cnbc.com/2024/05/20/scarlett-johansson-openai-chatgpt-sky.html.
Firt, Erez. 2024. What Makes Full Artificial Agents Morally Different. *AI & Society.* https://doi.org/10.1007/s00146-024-01867-6.
Foster, Raisa, Jussi Mäkelä, and Rebecca Martusewicz, eds. 2019. *Art, Ecojustice, and Education: Intersecting Theories and Practices.* London: Routledge.
Freire, Paulo. 1985. *Pedagogy of the Oppressed.* New York, NY: Penguin.
Gabriel, Iason, Arianna Manzini, Geoff Keeling, Lisa A. Hendricks, Verena Rieser, Hasan Iqbal, Nenad Tomašev, Ira Ktena, Zachary Kenton, Mikel Rodriguez, Seliem El-Sayed, Sasha Brown, Canfer Akbulut, Andrew Trask, Edward A. Hughes, Stevie Bergman, Renee Shelby, Nahema Marchal, Conor Griffin, Juan Mateos-Garcia, Victoria Krakovna, John O. Siy, Zeb Kurth-Nelson, Amand McCroskery, Vijay Bolina, Harry Law, Murray Shanahan, Lize Alberts, Borja Balle, Sarah de Haas, Yetunde Ibitoye, Allan Dafoe, Beth Goldberg, Sébastien Krier, Alexander Reese, Sims Witherspoon, Will Hawkins, Maribeth Rauh, Don Wallace, Matij Franklin, Josh A. Goldstein, Joel Lehman, Michael Klenk, Shannon Vallor, Courtney Biles, Meredith R. Morris, Helen King, Blaise Agüera y Arcas, William Isaac, and James Manyika. 2024. The Ethics of Advanced AI Assistants. https://arxiv.org/abs/2404.16244.
Gao, Didei, Lei Ji, Luowei Zhou, Kevin Q. Lin, Joya Chen, Zihan Fan, and Mike Z. Shou. 2023. AssistGPT: A General Multi-modal Assistant That Can Plan, Execute, Inspect, and Learn. https://doi.org/10.48550/ARXIV.2306.08640.
Gates, Bill. 2023. The Age of AI Has Begun. *GatesNotes*, 21 March. https://www.gatesnotes.com/The-Age-of-AI-Has-Begun.

Gibert, Martin, and Dominic Martin. 2022. In Search of the Moral Status of AI: Why Sentience Is a Strong Argument. *AI & Society* 37 (1): 319–330. https://doi.org/10.1007/s00146-021-01179-z.

Giddens, Anthony. 1997. *The Consequences of Modernity*. Redwood City, CA: Stanford University Press.

Gilbert, Thomas K., Megan W. Brozek, and Andrew Brozek. 2023. Beyond Bias and Compliance: Towards Individual Agency and Plurality of Ethics in AI. https://doi.org/10.48550/ARXIV.2302.12149.

Godfrey-Smith, Peter. 2002. Dewey on Naturalism, Realism and Science. *Philosophy of Science* 69 (S3): S25–S35. https://doi.org/10.1086/341765.

Gomede, Everton. 2024. AIcene: A New Epoch in Human History. *Medium*, 25 August. https://medium.com/the-modern-scientist/aicene-a-new-epoch-in-human-history-9793f443d2d9.

Goodchild, Simon, and Bharath Sriraman. 2012. Revisiting the Didactic Triangle: From the Particular to the General. *ZDM* 44 (5): 581–585. https://doi.org/10.1007/s11858-012-0449-3.

Gordon, John-Stewart, and Ausrine Pasvenskiene. 2021. Human Rights for Robots? A Literature Review. *AI and Ethics* 1 (4): 579–591. https://doi.org/10.1007/s43681-021-00050-7.

Gould, Julie. 2023. Art and Science: Close Cousins or Polar Opposites? *Nature*, 3 November. https://doi.org/10.1038/d41586-023-03389-5.

Graves, Stephen. 2024. Musician Imogen Heap Is Offering AI-Powered 'Songs as a Service'. *RScene*, 19 November. https://decrypt.co/292291/musician-imogen-heap-ai-song-service.

Grundy, S. 1987. *Curriculum: Product or Praxis?* Milton Park: Routledge.

Harari, Yuval Noah. 2024. *Nexus: A Brief History of Information Networks from the Stone Age to AI*. New York, NY: Random House.

Haraway, Donna J. 1991. A Cyborg Manifesto: Science, Technology, and Socialist-Feminism in the Late Twentieth Century. In *Simians, Cyborgs and Women: The Reinvention of Nature*, 149–182. New York, NY: Routledge.

Harman, Graham. 2002. *Tool-Being: Heidegger and the Metaphysics of Objects*. Chicago, IL: Open Court.

Harris, Daniel, and Stacy Holman Jones. 2022. A Manifesto for Posthuman Creativity Studies. *Qualitative Inquiry* 28 (5): 522–530. https://doi.org/10.1177/10778004211066632.

Harris, Jamie, and Jacy R. Anthis. 2021. The Moral Consideration of Artificial Entities: A Literature Review. *Science and Engineering Ethics* 27:53. https://doi.org/10.1007/s11948-021-00331-8.

Hatzius, Jan, Joseph Briggs, Devesh Kodnani, and Giovanni Pieromenico. 2023. The Potentially Large Effects of Artificial Intelligence on Economic Growth (Briggs/Kodnani). *Goldman Sachs*, 26 March. https://static.poder360.com.br/2023/03/Global-Economics-Analyst_-The-Potentially-Large-Effects-of-Artificial-Intelligence-on-Economic-Growth-Briggs_Kodnani.pdf.

Hawkins, Amy. 2024. Chinese Mourners Turn to AI to Remember and 'Revive' Loved Ones. *Guardian*, 4 April. https://www.theguardian.com/technology/2024/apr/04/chinese-mourners-turn-to-ai-to-remember-and-revive-loved-ones.

Heidegger, Martin. 2010. *Being and Time*. Albany, NY: State University of New York Press.

Heinrichs, Harald, and Frank Biermann. 2016. Sustainability: Politics and Governance. In *Sustainability Science*, ed. Harald Heinrichs, Pim Martens, Gerd Michelsen, and Arnim Wiek, 129–137. Dodrecht: Springer. https://doi.org/10.1007/978-94-017-7242 6_11.

Heras, Maria. 2022. Art and Connectedness Within Sustainability: Educating Through Aesthetic Pedagogies. In *Competences in Education for Sustainable Development*, ed. Paul Vare, Nadia Lausselet, and Marco Rieckmann, 145–157. Cham: Springer. https://doi.org/10.1007/978-3-030-91055-6_18.

Hiatt, Brian. 2023. Ready to Sing Elvis Karaoke...as Elvis? The Weird Rise of AI Music. *Rolling Stone*, 28 June. https://www.rollingstone.com/music/music-features/ai-music-drake-weeknd-ghostwriter977-beatles-elvis-voice-1234770094/.

Hickman, Larry A. 1992. *John Dewey's Pragmatic Technology*. Bloomington, IN: Indiana University Press.

———. 2001. *Philosophical Tools for Technological Culture: Putting Pragmatism to Work*. Bloomington, IN: Indiana University Press.

Hickman, Larry A. 2013. John Dewey's Legacy for the 21st Century. https://deweypragmatismo.wordpress.com/wp-content/uploads/2014/05/john-deweys-legacy-for-the-21st-larry-hickman.pdf.

Hilder, Thoma R. 2012. Repatriation, Revival and Transmission: The Politics of a Sámi Musical Heritage. *Ethnomusicology Forum* 21 (2): 161–179. https://doi.org/10.1080/17411912.2012.689473.

Hisariya, Tanisha, Huan Zhang, and Jinhua Liang. 2024. Bridging Paintings and Music—Exploring Emotion based Music Generation Through Paintings. https://doi.org/10.48550/arXiv.2409.07827.

Hutiri, Wiebke, Orestis Papakyriakopoulos, and Alice Xiang. 2024. Not My Voice! A Taxonomy of Ethical and Safety Harms of Speech Generators. In *The 2024 ACM Conference on Fairness, Accountability, and Transparency*, 359–376. New York, NY: Association for Computing Machinery. https://doi.org/10.1145/3630106.3658911.

Hutson, James, and Peter Cotroneo. 2023. Generative AI Tools in Art Education: Exploring Prompt Engineering and Iterative Processes for Enhanced Creativity. *Metaverse* 4 (1): 1–14. https://doi.org/10.54517/m.v4i1.2164.

Illeris, Helene. 2012. Interrogations: Art, Art Education and Environmental Sustainability. *International Journal of Education Through Art* 8 (3): 221–237. https://doi.org/10.1386/eta.8.3.221_1.

Ingham, Tim. 2023. Universal Music Group Responds to 'Fake Drake' AI Track: Streaming Platforms Have a Fundamental Responsibility to Prevent the Use of Their Services in Ways That Harm Artists. *Music Business Worldwide*, 17 April. https://www.musicbusinessworldwide.com/universal-music-group-responds-to-fake-drake-ai-track-streaming-platforms-have-a-fundamental-responsibility/.

Inwood, Hilary J., and Ryan W. Taylor. 2012. Creative Approaches to Environmental Learning: Two Perspectives on Teaching Environmental Art Education. *International Electronic Journal of Environmental Education* 2 (1): 65–75. https://files.eric.ed.gov/fulltext/EJ1057521.pdf.

Jain, Harshita, Renu Dhupper, Anamika Shrivastava, Deepak Kumar, and Maya Kumari. 2023. AI-Enabled Strategies for Climate Change Adaptation: Protecting Communities, Infrastructure, and Businesses from the Impacts of Climate Change. *Computational Urban Science* 3:25. https://doi.org/10.1007/s43762-023-00100-2.

Jeong, Heisawn, and Cindy E. Hmelo-Silver. 2016. Seven Affordances of Computer-Supported Collaborative Learning: How to Support Collaborative Learning? How Can Technologies Help? *Educational Psychologist* 51 (2): 247–265. https://doi.org/10.1080/00461520.2016.1158654.

Jeronen, Eila. 2020. Economic Sustainability. In *Encyclopedia of Sustainable Management*, ed. Samuel Idowu, Rene Schmidpeter, Nicholas Capaldi, Liangrong Zu, Mara Del Baldo, and Rute Abreu, 1–6. Cham: Springer. https://doi.org/10.1007/978-3-030-02006-4_197-1.

John-Steiner, Vera. 2006. *Creative Collaboration*. New York, NY: Oxford University Press. https://doi.org/10.1093/acprof:oso/9780195307702.001.0001.

Josan, Harnoovir S. 2023. AI and Deepfake Voice Cloning: Innovation, Copyright and Artists' Rights. Digital Policy Hub Working Paper. Waterloo: Centre for International Governance Innovation. https://www.cigionline.org/static/documents/DPH-paper-Josan.pdf.

Kemmis, Stephen, and Tracey J. Smith, eds. 2008. *Enabling Praxis: Challenges for Education*. Rotterdam: Sense.

King, Andrew. 2008. Collaborative Learning in the Music Studio. *Music Education Research* 10 (3): 423–438. https://doi.org/10.1080/14613800802280167.

Knox, Jeremy. 2019. What Does the 'Postdigital' Mean for Education? Three Critical Perspectives on the Digital, with Implications for Educational Research and Practice. *Postdigital Science and Education* 1 (2): 357–370. https://doi.org/10.1007/s42438-019-00045-y.

Kondor, Zsuzanna. 2016. New Media, Old Concerns: Heidegger Revisited. In *Philosophy of Emerging Media*, ed. Juliet Floyd and James E. Katz, 132–145. New York, NY: Oxford University Press. https://doi.org/10.1093/acprof:oso/9780190260743.003.0008.

Ladak, Ali, Jamie Harris, and Jacy R. Anthis. 2024. Which Artificial Intelligences Do People Care About Most? A Conjoint Experiment on Moral Consideration. https://doi.org/10.48550/ARXIV.2403.09405.

Lanier, Jaron. 2023. What My Musical Instruments Have Taught Me. *The New Yorker*, 22 July. https://www.newyorker.com/culture/the-weekend-essay/what-my-musical-instruments-have-taught-me.

Lara, Francisco, and Jarn Deckers, eds. 2023. *Ethics of Artificial Intelligence*. Cham: Springer. https://doi.org/10.1007/978-3-031-48135-2.

Latour, Bruno. 2005. *Reassembling the Social: An Introduction to Actor-Network-Theory*. Oxford: Oxford University Press.

Leonard, Nicholas. 2020. Entanglement Art Education: Factoring ARTificial Intelligence and Nonhumans into Future Art Curricula. *Art Education* 73 (4): 22–28. https://doi.org/10.1080/00043125.2020.1746163.

Li, Deyi, Wen He, and Yike Guo. 2021. Why AI Still Doesn't Have Consciousness? *CAAI Transactions on Intelligence Technology* 6 (2): 175–179. https://doi.org/10.1049/cit2.12035.

Li, Han, and Renwen Zhang. 2024. Finding Love in Algorithms: Deciphering the Emotional Contexts of Close Encounters with AI Chatbots. *Journal of Computer-Mediated Communication* 29 (5): zmae015. https://doi.org/10.1093/jcmc/zmae015.

Li, Pengfei, Jianyi Yang, Mohammad A. Islam, and Shaolei Ren. 2023. Making AI Less "Thirsty": Uncovering and Addressing the Secret Water Footprint of AI Models. https://doi.org/10.48550/ARXIV.2304.03271.

Lin, Rem R., Yongen Ke, and Kang Zhang. 2023. Urban Symphony: An AI and Data-Driven Approach to Real-Time Animation for Public Digital Art. In *Proceedings of the 16th International Symposium on Visual Information Communication and Interaction*, ed. Roger Malina, Zhang Kang, Zheng Wei, and Günter Wallner, 1–7. https://doi.org/10.1145/3615522.3615553.

Long, Zhang. 2024. A Father's Love: Musician "Revives" Daughter Using AI. *SHINE News*, 29 February. https://www.shine.cn/news/nation/2402292188/.

Looby, Christopher. 1996. *Voicing America: Language, Literary form, and the Origins of the United States*. Chicago, IL: University of Chicago Press.

Loxley, James. 2007. *Performativity*. London: Routledge.

Luccioni, Alexandra S., Yacine Jernite, and Emma Strubell. 2023. Power Hungry Processing: Watts Driving the Cost of AI Deployment? https://doi.org/10.48550/ARXIV.2311.16863.

Lundberg, Ebba, and Peter Mozelius. 2024. The Potential Effects of Deepfakes on News Media and Entertainment. *AI & Society*. https://doi.org/10.1007/s00146-024-02072-1.

Lyotard, Jean-François. 1984. *The Postmodern Condition: A Report on Knowledge*. Minneapolis, MN: University of Minnesota Press.

Mai, Kimberly T., Sergi Bray, Tob Davies, and Lewis D. Griffin. 2023. Warning: Humans Cannot Reliably Detect Speech Deepfakes. *PLOS ONE* 18 (8): e0285333. https://doi.org/10.1371/journal.pone.0285333.

Männistö-Funk, Tiina, and Tanja Sihvonen. 2018. Voices from the Uncanny Valley. *Digital Culture & Society* 4 (1): 45–64. https://doi.org/10.14361/dcs-2018-0105.

Mantoan, Diego. 2021. Sustainability Way Beyond Academia Public Art as a Driver for Behavioural Change and the Participatory Quest of Gayle Chong Kwan: Public Art as a Driver for Behavioural Change and the Participatory Quest of Gayle Chong Kwan. In *Waste Matters Chronicles from a Food Archipelago in Venice*, I libri di Ca' Foscari, 15–29. Venezia: Fondazione Università Ca' Foscari. https://doi.org/10.30687/978-88-6969-576-6/001.

Masood, Momina, Mariam Nawaz, Khalid M. Malik, Ali Javed, Aun Irtaza, and Hazif Malik. 2023. Deepfakes Generation and Detection: State-of-the-Art, Open Challenges, Countermeasures, and Way Forward. *Applied Intelligence* 53 (4): 3974–4026. https://doi.org/10.1007/s10489-022-03766-z.

Mekonnen, Habtamu, Zemenu Bires, and Kessegn Berhanu. 2022. Practices and Challenges of Cultural Heritage Conservation in Historical and Religious Heritage Sites: Evidence from North Shoa Zone, Amhara Region, Ethiopia. *Heritage Science* 10 (1): 172. https://doi.org/10.1186/s40494-022-00802-6.

Miettinen, Reijo. 2020. Hegel's Political and Social Theory: Ethical Life (Sittlichkeit) as a Historical-Institutional Context of Human Development. *Mind, Culture, and Activity* 27 (4): 360–372. https://doi.org/10.1080/10749039.2020.1725059.

Miller, Arthur I. 2019. *The Artist in the Machine: The World of AI-Powered Creativity*. Cambridge, MA: The MIT Press.

Mills, Kathy A., and Len Unsworth. 2017. Multimodal Literacy. In *Oxford Research Encyclopedia of Education*, ed. K.A. Mills and L. Unsworth. Oxford: Oxford University Press. https://doi.org/10.1093/acrefore/9780190264093.013.232.

Mills, Kelly, Pati Ruiz, Keun-woo Lee, Merjike Coenraad, Judi Fusco, Jeremy Roschelle, and Josh Weisgrau. 2024. AI Literacy: A Framework to Understand, Evaluate, and Use Emerging Technology. *Digital Promise*. https://doi.org/10.51388/20.500.12265/218.

Miyazaki, Shintaro. 2012. Algorhythmics: Understanding Micro-Temporality in Computational Cultures. *Computational Culture* 2. http://computationalculture.net/algorhythmics-understanding-micro-temporality-in-computational-cultures/.

More, Max. 1990. Transhumanism: Towards a Futuristic Philosophy. https://www.ildodopensiero.it/wp-content/uploads/2019/03/max-more-transhumanism-towards-a-futurist-philosophy.pdf.

Mori, Mahairo, Karl MacDorman, and Norri Kageki. 2012. The Uncanny Valley [From the Field]. *IEEE Robotics & Automation Magazine* 19 (2): 98–100. https://doi.org/10.1109/MRA.2012.2192811.

Napolitano, Domenico. 2023. The Shaping of The Shaping of a Standard Voice: Sonic and Sociotechnical Imaginaries in Smart Speakers. *Imago* 12 (21): 177–196. https://cab.unime.it/journals/index.php/IMAGO/article/view/3908.

Nasukawa, Kuniya. 2005. *A Unified Approach to Nasality and Voicing*. Berlin: De Gruyter. https://doi.org/10.1515/9783110910490.

Nazneen, Sohela, and Sultan Maheen. 2014. *Voicing Demands: Feminist Activism in Transnational Contexts*. New York, NY: Bloomsbury.

Ng, Davy T. K., Jac K. L. Leung, Samuel K. W. Chu, and Maggie S. Qiao. 2021. Conceptualizing AI Literacy: An Exploratory Review. *Computers and Education: Artificial Intelligence* 2:100041. https://doi.org/10.1016/j.caeai.2021.100041.

Nordgren, Anders. 2023. Artificial Intelligence and Climate Change: Ethical Issues. *Journal of Information, Communication and Ethics in Society* 21 (1): 1–15. https://doi.org/10.1108/JICES-11-2021-0106.

Nordström, Paulina, Riina Lundman, and Johanna Hautala. 2023. Evolving Coagency Between Artists and AI in the Spatial Cocreative Process of Artmaking. *Annals of the American Association of Geographers* 113 (9): 2203–2218. https://doi.org/10.1080/24694452.2023.2210647.

Open AI. 2024. How the Voices for ChatGPT Were Chosen, 19 May. https://openai.com/index/how-the-voices-for-chatgpt-were-chosen/.

Open letter to President Biden from tech workers in Kenya. 2024, 22 May. https://www.foxglove.org.uk/open-letter-to-president-biden-from-tech-workers-in-kenya.

Østern, Anna-Lena, and Kristian N. Knudsen, eds. 2020. *Performative Approaches in Arts Education: Artful Teaching, Learning, and Research*. London: Routledge.

Pareschi, Remo. 2024a. Beyond Human and Machine: An Architecture and Methodology Guideline for Centaurian Design. *Sci* 6 (4): 71. https://doi.org/10.3390/sci6040071.

———. 2024b. *Centaur Art: The Future of Art in the Age of Generative AI*. Cham: Springer. https://doi.org/10.1007/978-3-031-69063-1.

Park, Sungijn. 2024. The Work of Art in the Age of Generative AI: Aura, Liberation, and Democratization. *AI & Society*. https://doi.org/10.1007/s00146-024-01948-6.

Park, Ye S. 2023. Creative and Critical Entanglements with AI in Art Education. *Studies in Art Education* 64 (4): 406–425. https://doi.org/10.1080/00393541.2023.2255084.

Partti, Heidi. 2014. Cosmopolitan Musicianship Under Construction: Digital Musicians Illuminating Emerging Values in Music Education. *International Journal of Music Education* 32 (1): 3–18. https://doi.org/10.1177/0255761411433727.

Partti, Heidi, and Sidsel Karlsen. 2010. Reconceptualising Musical Learning: New Media, Identity and Community in Music Education. *Music Education Research* 12 (4): 369–382. https://doi.org/10.1080/14613808.2010.519381.

Paulus, Paul B., and Bernard A. Nijstad, eds. 2019. *The Oxford Handbook of Group Creativity and Innovation*. Oxford: Oxford University Press. https://doi.org/10.1093/oxfordhb/9780190648077.001.0001.

Pavlou, Victoria. 2024. *Critical ARts Education for Sustainable Societies: A Handbook for Arts Educators*. Cyprus: Frederick University.

Pejcha, Camille S. 2022. Who Does Your Voice Belong To? For Musician Holly Herndon, the Answer Is 'Everyone'. *Document*, 27 January. https://www.documentjournal.com/2022/01/who-does-your-voice-belong-to-for-musician-holly-herndon-the-answer-is-everyone/.

Pinski, Marc, and Alexander Benlian. 2024. AI Literacy for Users—A Comprehensive Review and Future Research Directions of Learning Methods, Components, and Effects. *Computers in Human Behavior: Artificial Humans* 2 (1): 100062. https://doi.org/10.1016/j.chbah.2024.100062.

Placani, Adriana. 2024. Anthropomorphism in AI: Hype and Fallacy. *AI and Ethics* 4 (3): 691–698. https://doi.org/10.1007/s43681-024-00419-4.

Ploin, Anne, Rebecca Eyonon, Isis Hjorth, and Michael A. Osborne. 2024. *AI and the Arts: How Machine Learning Is Changing Artistic Work. Report from the Creative Algorithmic Intelligence Research Project*. Oxford: University of Oxford. https://www.oii.ox.ac.uk/wp-content/uploads/2022/03/040222-AI-and-the-Arts_FINAL.pdf.

Poole, Steven. 2024. Nexus by Yuval Noah Harari Review—End of Days? *The Guardian*, 11 September. https://www.theguardian.com/books/article/2024/sep/11/nexus-by-yuval-noah-harari-review-the-ai-apocalypse.

Purvis, Ben, Yong Mao, and Darren Robinson. 2019. Three Pillars of Sustainability: In Search of Conceptual Origins. *Sustainability Science* 14 (3): 681–695. https://doi.org/10.1007/s11625-018-0627-5.

Raman, Raghu, Debidutta Pattnaik, Hiran H. Lathabai, Chandan Kumar, Kannan Govindan, and Prema Nedungadi. 2024. Green and Sustainable AI Research: An Integrated Thematic and Topic Modeling Analysis. *Journal of Big Data* 11:55. https://doi.org/10.1186/s40537-024-00920-x.

Ramati, Ido. 2024. Algorithmic Ventriloquism: The Contested State of Voice in AI Speech Generators. *Social Media + Society* 10 (1): https://doi.org/10.1177/20563051231224401.

Ramsøy, Thomas Z. 2024. The Misunderstood Musings of AI: Confabulation, Not Hallucination. https://thomasramsoy.com/index.php/2024/03/12/the-misunderstood-musings-of-ai-confabulation-not-hallucination/.

Rancière, Jacques. 1999. *Disagreement: Politics and Philosophy*. Minneapolis, MN: University of Minnesota Press.

———. 2004. *The Politics of Aesthetics: The Distribution of the Sensible*. London: Continuum.

———. 2012. *Aisthesis: Scenes from the Aesthetic Regime of Art*. London: Verso.

Reben, Alexander. 2019. AmalGAN. https://areben.com/project/amalgan/.

Reckwitz, Andreas. 2017. *The Invention of Creativity: Modern Society and the Culture of the New*. Cambridge: Polity.

———. 2020a. *The Society of Singularities*. Boston: De Gruyter.

———. 2020b. The Society of Singularities. In *Futures of the Study of Culture: Interdisciplinary Perspectives, Global Challenges*, ed. Doris Bachmann-Medick, Jens Kugele, and Ansgar Nünning, 141–154. Berlin: De Gruyter.

———. 2021. *The End of Illusions: Politics, Economy, and Culture in Late Modernity*. Cambridge: Polity.

Rehding, Alexander. 2024. J.S. Bach, Musicology/Music Theory, and AI: Convergences and Divergences Between Disciplines. A paper presentation at *The First International Conference in AI Music Studies*, Stockholm, December 12.

Reigeluth, Tyler. 2023. Machine Learning Normativity as Performativity. In *Handbook of Critical Studies of Artificial Intelligence*, ed. S. Lindgren, 584–594. Cheltenham: Edward Elgar Publishing. https://doi.org/10.4337/9781803928562.00060.

Report of the World Commission on Environment and Development: Our Common Future. 1987. https://sustainabledevelopment.un.org/content/documents/5987our-common-future.pdf.

Rezat, Sebastian, and Rudolf Sträßer. 2012. From the Didactical Triangle to the Socio-Didactical Tetrahedron: Artifacts as Fundamental Constituents of the Didactical Situation. *ZDM* 44 (5): 641–651. https://doi.org/10.1007/s11858-012-0448-4.

Rinaldi, Ivan, Nicola Fanelli, Giovanna Castellano, and Gennaro Vessio. 2024. Art2Mus: Bridging Visual Arts and Music Through Cross-Modal Generation. 10.48550/arXiv.2410.04906.

Rouse, Joseph. 2004. Barad's Feminist Naturalism. *Hypatia* 19 (1): 142–161. https://doi.org/10.1111/j.1527-2001.2004.tb01272.x.

Ruthven, Kenneth. 2012. The Didactical Tetrahedron as a Heuristic for Analysing the Incorporation of Digital Technologies Into Classroom Practice in Support of Investigative Approaches to Teaching Mathematics. *ZDM* 44 (5): 627–640. https://doi.org/10.1007/s11858-011-0376-8.

Salonen, Arto O., and Marjatta Brady. 2015. Ekososiaalinen sivistys herättää luottamusta tulevaisuuteen [Ecosocial *Bildung* Raises Trust in the Future]. *Aikuiskasvatus* 35 (1): 4–15. https://doi.org/10.33336/aik.94118.

Salonen, Arto O., and Jyrki Konkka. 2015. An Ecosocial Approach to Well-Being: A Solution to the Wicked Problems in the Era of Anthropocene. *Foro de*

Educación 13 (19): 19–34. https://www.redalyc.org/pdf/4475/447544537003.pdf.

Saner, Emine. 2024. Inside the Taylor Swift Deepfake Scandal: 'It's Men Telling a Powerful Woman to Get Back in Her Box'. *The Guardian*, 31 January. https://www.theguardian.com/technology/2024/jan/31/inside-the-taylor-swift-deepfake-scandal-its-men-telling-a-powerful-woman-to-get-back-in-her-box.

Schaffar, Birgit, and Lili-Ann Wolff. 2024. Phenomenon-Based Learning in Finland: A Critical Overview of Its Historical and Philosophical Roots. *Cogent Education* 11 (1): 2309733. https://doi.org/10.1080/2331186X.2024.2309733.

Schütz, Alfred, and Thomas Luckmann. 1973. *The Structures of the Life-World*. Vol. 1. Evanston, IL: Northwestern University Press.

Sedgwick, Eve K. 2003. *Touching Feeling: Affect, Pedagogy, Performativity*. Durham, NC: Duke University Press. https://doi.org/10.1215/9780822384786.

Seigfried, Charlene H., ed. 2001. *Feminist Interpretations of John Dewey*. University Park, PN: Pennsylvania State University Press.

Sharma, Shalini. 2023. Cultivating Pedagogical Sustainability in Early Education. *International Journal of Management Education for Sustainable Development* 6 (6): 13–23. https://ijsdcs.com/index.php/IJMESD/article/view/320.

Shook, John R. 2017. The Nature Philosophy of John Dewey. *Dewey Studies* 1 (1): 13–43. http://www.pragmatism.org/shook/2017%20Shook%20The%20Nature%20Philosophy%20of%20John%20Dewey.pdf.

Shu, Lee-Lean. 2024. The Untold Story of AI's Huge Carbon Footprint. *Forbes*, 26 April. https://www.forbes.com/councils/forbestechcouncil/2024/04/26/the-untold-story-of-ais-huge-carbon-footprint/.

Siljander, Pauli, Ari Kivelä, and Ari Sutinen, eds. 2012. *Theories of Bildung and Growth: Connections and Controversies Between Continental Educational Thinking and American Pragmatism*. Rotterdam: Sense.

Sjöström, Jesper, and Ingo Eilks. 2021. The Bildung Theory—From von Humboldt to Klafki and Beyond. In *Science Education in Theory and Practice*, ed. Ben Akpan and Teresa J. Kennedy. Cham: Springer. https://link.springer.com/chapter/10.1007/978-3-030-43620-9_5.

Smith, Ralph A. 2008. Educational Aesthetics and Policy. *Arts Education Policy Review* 109 (6): 3–12. https://doi.org/10.3200/AEPR.109.6.3-12.

Soini, Katriina, and Inger Birkeland. 2014. Exploring the Scientific Discourse on Cultural Sustainability. *Geoforum* 51:213–223. https://doi.org/10.1016/j.geoforum.2013.12.001.

Souza-Rodrigues, Eduardo. 2019. Deforestation in the Amazon: A Unified Framework for Estimation and Policy Analysis. *The Review of Economic Studies* 86 (6): 2713–2744. https://doi.org/10.1093/restud/rdy070.

Stahl, Bernd C., Doris Schroeder, and Rowena Rodrigues. 2023. *Ethics of Artificial Intelligence: Case Studies and Options for Addressing Ethical Challenges.* Cham: Springer. https://link.springer.com/book/10.1007/978-3-031-17040-9.

Stano, Simona. 2019. The Corporeal Meaning of Language: A Semiotic Approach to Musical Glossolalia. *Semiotica* 2019 (229): 69–85. https://doi.org/10.1515/sem-2018-0091.

Stephenson, Janet. 2023. *Culture and Sustainability: Exploring Stability and Transformation with the Cultures Framework.* Cham: Springer. https://doi.org/10.1007/978-3-031-25515-1.

Stiegler, Bernard. 2019. *The Age of Disruption: Technology and Madness in Computational Capitalism.* Cambridge: Polity.

Stroud, Scott R. 2011. *John Dewey and the Artful Life: Pragmatism, Aesthetics, and Morality.* University Park, PN: Pennsylvania State University Press.

Sturm, Bob L. T., Ken Déguernel, Rujing S. Huang, Andre Holzapfel, Ollie Bown, Nick Collins, Jonathan Sterne, Laura Cros Vida, Luca Casini, David Dalmazzo, Eric Drott, and Odedin Ben-Tal. 2024. MusAIcology: AI Music and the Need for a New Kind of Music Studies. https://doi.org/10.31235/osf.io/9pz4x.

Sui, Peiqi, Eamon Duede, Sophie Wu, and Richard J. So. 2024. Confabulation: The Surprising Value of Large Language Model Hallucinations. https://doi.org/10.48550/ARXIV.2406.04175.

Suno. 2024. Answer of Defendant Suno, Inc. to Complaint. 1 August. https://www.musicbusinessworldwide.com/files/2024/08/SUNO-response-to-copyright-suit.pdf.

Tall, David. 1986. Using the Computer as an Environment for Building and Testing Mathematical Concepts. In *Intelligence, Learning and Understanding in Mathematics: A Tribute to Richard Skemp*, ed. David Tall and Michael Thomas, 21–36. Post Pressed.

Tavin, Kevin, Gila Kolb, and Juuso Tervo, ed. 2021. *Post-Digital, Post-Internet Art and Education: The Future is All-Over.* Cham: Springer.

Tietäväinen, Ville. 2024. Olemme luomassa epookkia, joka muuttaa historian irvikuvakseen [We Are Creating an Epoch That Changes History to Its Mockery]. *Helsingin Sanomat*, 17 December. https://www.hs.fi/mielipide/art-2000010905128.html.

Toivonen, Hannu. 2023. *Mitä tekoäly on? [What AI Is?]* Helsinki: Teos.

Touraine, Alain. 1971. *The Post-industrial society: Tomorrow's Social History: Classes, Conflicts, and Culture in the Programmed Society.* New York, NY: Random House.

Trillo, Roberto A., and Malek Poliks, eds. 2024. *Choreomata: Performance and Performativity After AI.* London: Routledge.

Trott, Carlie D., Trevor L. Even, and Susan M. Frame. 2020. Merging the Arts and Sciences for Collaborative Sustainability Action: A Methodological

Framework. *Sustainability Science* 15 (4): 1067–1085. https://doi.org/10.1007/s11625-020-00798-7.

Vaccari, Cristian, and Andrew Chadwick. 2020. Deepfakes and Disinformation: Exploring the Impact of Synthetic Political Video on Deception, Uncertainty, and Trust in News. *Social Media + Society* 6 (1): 205630512090340. https://doi.org/10.1177/2056305120903408.

Vacchi, Marco, Cristina Siligardi, Fabio Demaria, Erika I. Cedillo-González, Rocio González-Sánchez, and Davide Settembre-Blundo. 2021. Technological Sustainability or Sustainable Technology? A Multidimensional Vision of Sustainability in Manufacturing. *Sustainability* 13 (17): 9942. https://doi.org/10.3390/su13179942.

Väkevä, Lauri. 2007. Art Education, The Art of Education and the Art of Life: Considering the Implications of Dewey's Later Philosophy to Art and Music Education. *Action, Criticism & Theory for Music Education* 6 (1): 1–15. https://act.maydaygroup.org/articles/Vakeva6_1.pdf.

———. 2012. Experiencing Growth as a Natural Phenomenon: John Dewey's Philosophy and the Bildung Tradition. In *Theories of Bildung and Growth*, ed. Pauli Siljader, Ari Kivelä, and Ari Sutinen, 261–279. Rotterdam: Sense.

———. 2019. Evaluation for Equality: Applying a Classical Pragmatist Perspective in Qualitative Assessment in Finnish General Music Education. In *The Oxford Handbook of Philosophical and Qualitative Assessment in Music Education*, ed. David J. Elliott, Marissa Silverman, and Gary E. McPherson, 100–121. New York, NY: Oxford University Press. https://doi.org/10.1093/oxfordhb/9780190265182.013.7.

———. 2023a. *Considering Deweyan Cultural Naturalism as a Philosophy of Art(s) Education: Restoring Continuity.* Cham: Springer. https://doi.org/10.1007/978-3-031-38817-0.

———. 2023b. Kestävyysajattelu musiikkikasvattajan ammatillisen refektiivisyyden haastajana [Challenging the Professional Reflectivity of Music Educator with Sustainability Thinking]. In *Musiikkikasvatus muutoksessa* [*Music Education in Transformation*], ed. Marja-Leena Juntunen, and Heidi Partti, 479–500. Helsinki: DocMus Research Publications 20, Sibelius Academy of the University of the Arts Helsinki. https://taju.uniarts.fi/bitstream/handle/10024/7961/e-pdf_Musiikkikasvatus%20muutoksessa_Sibelius-Akatemia.pdf?sequence=1&isAllowed=y.

———. 2024. Limits of Text-Based Prompting in Multimodal AI Models: Theoretical Implications for Art(s) Education. A paper presentation at *AIRiAL 2024 Conference*, Teachers College, Columbia University, New York (NY), 27 September.

Väkevä, Lauri, and Heidi Partti. 2025 (in print). Towards AI Didactics: Call for Teachers to Train Large Language Models for Research Writing in Higher Arts

Education. In *Education and Artificial Intelligence Handbook*, ed. Guy Tchibozo. Cham: Springer.

Väkevä, Lauri, and Katja Thomson. 2025. Turvallinen tila taiteen korkeakoulutuksessa [Safe Space in Higher Art Education]. In *Erimielisten tila: Vaikeiden aiheiden käsittely opetuksessa* [*Space of Disagreement: Handling Difficult Topics in Teaching*], ed. Mikko Puustinen, Jenni Marjokorpi, and Janne Säntti, 95–110. Helsinki: Gaudemus.

Van Manen, Max. 1991. *The Tact of Teaching: The Meaning of Pedagogical Thoughtfulness*. Albany, NY: State University of New York Press.

———. 2015. *Pedagogical tact: Knowing What to Do When You Don't Know What to Do*. Milton Park: Routledge.

Van Wynsberghe, Aimee. 2021. Sustainable AI: AI for Sustainability and the Sustainability of AI. *AI and Ethics* 1 (3): 213–218. https://doi.org/10.1007/s43681-021-00043-6.

Verdecchia, Roberto, June Sallou, and Luis Cruz. 2023. A Systematic Review of Green AI. https://doi.org/10.48550/ARXIV.2301.11047.

Vinge, Vernor. 1993. The Coming Technological Singularity: How to Survive in the Post-Human Era. https://edoras.sdsu.edu/~vinge/misc/singularity.html.

Voigts, Eckart, Robin M. Auer, Dietmar Elflein, Sebastian Kunas, Jan Röhnert, and Christop Seelinger, eds. 2024a. *Artificial Intelligence—Intelligent Art?: Human-Machine Interaction and Creative Practice*. Bielefeld: transcript. https://doi.org/10.14361/9783839469224.

Voigts, Eckart, Dietmar Elflein, and Jan Röhnert. 2024b. Artificial Intelligence – Intelligent Art? An Introduction. In *Artificial Intelligence – Intelligent Art? Human-Machine Interaction and Creative Practice*, ed. Eckart Voigts, Robin M. Auer, Dietmar Elflein, Sebastian Kunas, Jan Röhnert, and Christop Seelinger, 9–34. Bielefeld: transcript. https://doi.org/10.14361/9783839469224.

Vorsino, M. 2015. Re-Reading Dewey Through a Feminist Lens. *Educational Perspectives* 47 (1–2): 50–54.

Wang, Ziie J., Robert Turko, Omar Shaikh, Haekyu Park, Nilaksh Das, Fred Hohman, Minsuk Kahng, and Duen H. Chau. 2020. CNN 101: Interactive Visual Learning for Convolutional Neural Networks. In *Extended Abstracts of the 2020 CHI Conference on Human Factors in Computing Systems*, 1–7. Honolulu, HI: Association for Computing Machinery. https://doi.org/10.1145/3334480.3382899.

Whitehead, Alfred N. 1978. *Process and Reality: An Essay in Cosmology. Gifford Lectures Delivered in the University of Edinburgh During the Session 1927–28*. New York, NY: The Free Press.

Whittlestone, Jess, and Samuel Clarke. 2022. AI Challenges for Society and Ethics. In *The Oxford Handbook of AI Governance*, ed. Justin B. Bullock, Yu-Che Chen, Johannes Himmelreich, Valerie M. Hudson, Anton Korinek, Matthew

M. Young, and Baobao Zhang, 45–64. New York, NY: Oxford University Press. https://doi.org/10.1093/oxfordhb/9780197579329.013.3.

Wiener, Anna. 2023. Holly Herndon's Infinite Art. *The New Yorker*, 13 November. https://www.newyorker.com/magazine/2023/11/20/holly-herndons-infinite-art.

Wiesner, Christian, Kerstin Zechner, and Simone Breit. 2023. The Didactic Triangle from Sign-Theoretical Perspectives to Deepen the Pedagogical Situation. A paper at *ECER 2023* Conference, 22 August. https://eera-ecer.de/ecer-programmes/conference/28/contribution/57908.

Wilks, Yorick, ed. 2010. *Close Engagements with Artificial Companions: Key Social, Psychological, Ethical and Design Issues*. Amsterdam: John Benjamins Publishing Company.

Wright, Benjamin. 2007. The Wilhelm Scream. *Offscreen* 11:8–9. https://offscreen.com/pdf/wright_forum1.pdf.

Wu, Carole-Jean, Ramya Raghavendra, Udit Gupta, Bilge Acun, Newsha Ardalani, Kiwan Maeng, Gloria Chang, Fiona A. Behram, James Huang, Charles Bai, Michael Gschwind, Anurag Gupta, Myle Ott, Anastasia Melnikov, Salvatire Candido, David Brooks, Geeta Chauhan, Benjamin Lee, Hsien-Hsin Lee, Akyildiz Bugra, Maximilian Balandat, Joe Spisak, Ravi Jain, Mike Rabbat, and Kim Hazelwood. 2021. Sustainable AI: Environmental Implications, Challenges and Opportunities. https://doi.org/10.48550/ARXIV.2111.00364.

Yin, Shukang, Chaoyu Fu, Shirui Zhao, Ke Li, Xing Sun, Tong Xu, and Enhong Chen. 2024. A Survey on Multimodal Large Language Models. *National Science Review* 11 (12): nwae403. https://doi.org/10.1093/nsr/nwae403.

Zheng, Qingxiau, and Yun Huang. 2023. The Self 2.0: How AI-Enhanced Self-Clones Transform Self-Perception and Improve Presentation Skills. http://arxiv.org/abs/2310.15112.

Zylinska, Joanna. 2020. *AI Art: Machine Visions and Warped Dreams*. London: Open Humanities Press.

Index[1]

[1] Note: Page numbers followed by 'n' refer to notes.

L. Väkevä, *Voicing Responsible AI Pedagogy for Music and Visual Arts Education*, https://doi.org/10.1007/978-3-031-86410-0

Kolibri 360 GmbH
Ferdinand-Jühlke-Straße 7
99095 Erfurt, Deutschland
produktsicherheit@kolibri360.de